SPIRIT

OF A

HUMMINGBIRD

MEMORIES FROM A
CHILDHOOD ON THE RUN

FELICIA THAI HEATH

RIVER GROVE
BOOKS

This book is a memoir reflecting the author's present recollections of experiences over time. Its story and its words are the author's alone. Some details and characteristics may be changed, some events may be compressed, and some dialogue may be recreated.

Published by River Grove Books
Austin, TX
www.rivergrovebooks.com

Distributed by River Grove Books

Design and composition by Greenleaf Book Group
Cover design by Greenleaf Book Group
Cover image: abstract oil paint texture on canvas, background; barbed wire prison fence; used under licence from Shutterstock.com

Publisher's Cataloging-in-Publication data is available.

Print ISBN: 978-1-63299-570-4

eBook ISBN: 978-1-63299-571-1

Audiobook ISBN: 978-1-63299-572-8

First Edition

For my mom, whose resilience gave me power

*To my husband, Ricky, whose love and
support made this book possible*

*To my children, Skylar, Maverick, Naomi,
and Zuri, who give me purpose*

PROLOGUE

"Unknown caller." The words flashed across my phone as it vibrated on my desk. I was in the middle of studying for my first medical board exam, so I let the call go to voicemail with a slight sense of relief. My voice mailbox was full, and I couldn't be bothered to clean it out.

I was in my third year of medical school and had been studying for this exam for weeks. It was still a month away, but I was determined to ace it since it would be the first of many to come in my future career. Plus I had a solid schedule that I diligently followed.

My day always started at 6:30 a.m. sharp. I'd take a fifteen-minute coffee break at ten, lunch at noon, and then study until five, before I'd hit the gym for one hour to defuse the stress, take my mind off the books, and sweat out any doubts. Then, I'd take a quick shower and have dinner, followed by a final sixty minutes of skimming through my notes, before calling it a night and resting up before another productive day.

I did this seven days a week, with no weekends off. My focus was unshakeable.

On that particular day, I ignored my phone and looped my hair back into a ponytail. I continued to read from where I left off, marking up my textbook with a highlighter and taking detailed notes. I rolled back and forth on my pink yoga ball, which I opted for instead of a desk chair. I'd heard that the movement and resultant blood circulation helped you stay more alert during extended study sessions.

As I challenged myself to memorize the material before turning the page, my phone buzzed again.

"Unknown Caller."

Irritated by the interruption, I silenced the vibration and unplugged the phone from the charger. Whoever it was, answering the call might be more efficient than letting it ring again.

I slid my thumb across the screen to answer. "Hello?" I said.

No answer.

"Hellooo?"

"Hello. You have a collect call from—" an operator recording on the other end intoned, followed by another voice: "Daddy. Felicia, it's your—" The voice was cut off. The recording resumed, "An inmate at the Federal Correctional Institution. To accept this call, please press pound. To reject this call, please hang up, and you will be disconnected."

I grunted. I had seconds to decide. I tapped the pound key. Years had gone by since I had last chosen pound over the red button. "Your call will be recorded."

"Felicia?" Dad's foreign voice gave me chills. He'd started calling me by my American name after he went away. My dad had been in prison for the last fifteen years after being convicted for conspiracy to commit murder among other charges. He had been arrested three years before his conviction and held without bail, ultimately pleading guilty at the end of his high-profile trial. It had been eighteen years since I had seen him.

"Hi."

"Wow, baby, it's so good to hear your voice. It's your daddy. How are you?"

"I'm good."

"Good. I've missed you so much, honey. I don't have much time on the phone. Have you been getting my letters?"

"Yeah, some of them." Some of them went into the trash unopened.

"Did you get the picture? Your daddy is getting old." He chuckled. "Do you even remember what I look like? I miss you every day, baby. I think about you every day. Listen, baby. I know you've been busy with medical school and haven't had a chance to visit me, but I have good news." Excitement was ramping up in his tone.

Dad had been transferred to multiple different prisons over the years to be as close to me as possible. First, it was from Indiana to Maryland when I was at James Madison University for my bachelor's degree. Then, he transferred to West Virginia when I was in Washington, DC, earning my master's. The shorter the distance between us, the more obligated I felt to go see him. Yet with each relocation, I convinced myself that it was still too inconvenient. I was too busy, the drive was too long, and the logistics of a federal prison visit were too complicated. Hidden in between my excuses was my vulnerability. I had no one to come with me, and as fiercely independent as I considered myself to be, facing my father as a grown woman was a feat I couldn't do alone. I pictured a flood of sorrow, resentment, and rage crashing through my composure and drowning every effort I put into moving forward gracefully. I wasn't sure if I was strong enough to endure the encounter and come up for air at the end of it. Ultimately, I knew it wasn't a risk I was willing to take. I had come too far, and he wasn't worth it.

I never made it out to see him before moving to an island in the West Indies for the academic portion of medical school. By the time I returned to the United States for the clinical part of my degree, we were completely out of touch.

Now, hearing his voice on the other end of the phone, I waited for his news.

"I'm getting out, baby! I'm getting out on good behavior," Dad said, sounding borderline proud.

My eyes bulged, and I halted the rolling yoga ball beneath me. "Really? You are? When?" I could've sworn he wasn't getting out for close to another decade. I had planned to visit. One day. Before those ten years were up.

"If everything's good, I'll be out in seven, eight months. A year at the most."

"Okay. How sure are you about this?" I went through the calendar in my head.

"I'm sure. My parole officer is working on it, too. Everything looks good so far. Tell your mommy, okay? And tell Amanda and Bryan that Dad's coming home."

"They don't know?"

"You tell them. Tell them I'm getting out. I'm coming home, and I'm going to take care of everything. We're going to be a family again."

"All of us? A family?" I repeated.

"Yes, Felicia. Daddy's coming home."

We hung up.

I launched myself off my yoga ball and flopped onto my bed. I stared at the ceiling wondering what had just happened.

A family again.

I repeated the phrase in my mind a few times. The first time, the thought left me feeling empty. They were just three meaningless words. The second time, I was disgusted. He was a liar, abusive, and, at most, a deadbeat father. There was nothing romantic about the idea of him reuniting with his three bastard children. A wave of nausea made me feel flushed. The third time, I wrinkled my forehead in bewilderment. Us, a family again? Was this like a second chance, a chance to be free of dysfunction and filled with love? The idea was painfully wonderful: a mother, a father, two daughters, and a son with a forgivable past and a future together.

1

"Go put on your jacket," Mom said as she rushed into the apartment.

"Where are we going?" I asked as I got up from the Lego-covered floor and approached the closet. I heard drawers slamming in the bedroom and panic in her footsteps. She still had her black boots on. We never wore shoes inside.

She came back out carrying a duffel bag.

"Come on. Where's your jacket? Put on your boots. Let's go." Her hands shook as she tried to align the zipper on my winter coat.

"Where are we going, Mommy?" I asked again.

Without a word, she shoved my boots onto my feet, and we left. Mom gripped the fabric on the arm of my shiny puffer jacket, yanking me down the hallway. My strides fell short of hers, and I tripped on the carpet. She pulled me harder so I could catch my next step.

When we got outside, it was almost dark, and a snow flurry

was making its way down to earth. A man who I knew only as "Uncle" opened the passenger door of a black Mercedes-Benz and waved for me to come. Mom gently passed me off to him, and he lifted me into the seat, buckled my seat belt, and closed the door. I felt the thump of the trunk being closed, and then, Mom appeared in the driver's seat.

Uncle was leaning into her open car window.

"He's with Sara. You should have a few hours," he said.

She made no response, and we sped off.

We drove for what felt like hours. Mom's hands clutched the steering wheel as tightly as a child's hands gripped the monkey bars at the park.

Eventually, I piped up. "I'm hungry, Mommy," I said.

"We're almost there. We can't stop yet."

"But where are we going?"

"We're going to stay with your Grandma Agnes for a little bit," she answered. Her neck was stiff, and her eyes never left the road.

"Who's that?"

"She's family."

"Okay." Her abrupt response meant no more questions. I drifted off as the white highway lines and the car's hum soothed me to sleep.

The brake of the car roused me. We were parked in the driveway of a charming gray house I had never seen before. Mom rubbed my head as I rubbed my eyes.

"Let's go inside and meet your grandparents," she whispered. Her eyebrows furrowed and her lips thinned into a nervous smile.

We got out of the car, and she went to the trunk and grabbed her bags while I waited in the driveway. The flurries had by now turned into feathery snowflakes as big as quarters. They gathered on my shoulders in clumps.

We rang the doorbell three times before a sleepy older couple answered the door.

"Hi, Mom," my own mother said.

They didn't look like my grandparents. As far as I knew, my only grandparents were Chinese. My petite Maa-Maa and my wise and wrinkled Yeh-Yeh, neither of whom spoke more than a word of English. A tall Caucasian woman with frizzy brown curls and a hooked nose squinted at us.

"Lon? What are you doing here?" the woman now asked as she tied her burgundy robe at her waist.

"Come inside," a man with hooded blue eyes and a humble face said as he opened the door further. He embraced Mom. Her body went limp, and she dropped the duffel bag.

"I have nowhere else to go. I drove here from the city. I need a place to stay. This is my daughter, Felicia," she explained, gesturing toward me. "This is your Grandma Agnes and Grandpa Martin, baby."

"Where's Peter?" Agnes asked, after giving me a blank glance, referring to my father.

I wondered the same thing.

Martin helped me to the couch. The cushions smelled like moth balls, and my feet dangled over an elegant antique rug. Pale teal wallpaper with efflorescent borders surrounded us, and a brass pendulum swung inside a mahogany longcase clock at the other end of the living room.

"He's still there. He was out working. We left him. He doesn't know we're here. His friends helped me escape, but I had nowhere to go, Mom."

"You can't stay here. He'll come looking for you," Agnes said, her voice rising.

"No, Mom, he won't know I'm here."

"He'll find you, Lon! You've put us all in danger!" Agnes's neck tensed. She blinked rapidly.

"You can stay," Martin interjected.

"No, they can't! They're not staying here, Martin," Agnes scolded.

"You're staying, honey. Let's get you settled in," Martin said in a sweet voice, coaxing Mom as if she were nine rather than nineteen.

"You're not staying here, Lon. You can't stay here. Peter has been all over the news. If he doesn't find you, the cops will."

"He won't. They won't. I promise. I didn't do anything wrong, Mom. The cops can't do anything to me. I swear," Mom said, nodding her head in distress.

"We're not talking about this. You need to get out. Get out of here right now!"

"But, Mom, I have all this money. You can have it. Just . . . please! I have nowhere to go. She's only three, and we have nowhere to go," Mom begged. She got down on the floor and unfastened the zipper of her duffel bag. Stacks of hundred-dollar bills bound with tight rubber bands were revealed.

"That money's dirty." Agnes narrowed her eyes and scanned the cash. "Put it away. You can't have that money in this house! He's going to come looking for it," Agnes said. She snatched up the bag, stomped to the door, and tossed the duffel bag onto the lawn.

"Are you crazy, Agnes? This is our daughter! Didn't you hear her? She has nowhere to go with her child, for God's sake! It's the middle of the night, and there's a blizzard out there. Let them stay for the night. We'll figure this out in the morning," Martin said, stepping between them.

I didn't know it at the time, but these new grandparents were named Agnes and Martin Schafer, and they were my mom's adoptive parents. Agnes was a math teacher at Hingham Junior High in Hingham, Massachusetts. Classy and conservative in nature, she was a woman of Christian faith and values. Martin was an easygoing guy with a sympathetic nature. He loved to sail and spent most of his leisure time on the deck. When their church learned of the Vietnamese "boat people" stranded in a Malaysian refugee camp, desperate to be sponsored or adopted by American families and rescued from their grave conditions, the members decided to come together and fundraise enough money to bring one family overseas. Mom was sponsored at the age of twelve and became a student at Agnes's school. After being poorly treated in one foster home after another during her first year in America, Agnes and Martin decided to adopt Mom, making her a younger sister to their own two daughters.

After Mom eloped with my dad on her fifteenth birthday, Martin had looked for her for months. Her runaway note claimed that she had located a family member from Vietnam and had gone to live with them. Martin knew better. He drove through the streets in Hingham and the surrounding towns with her photo in hand, searching for his Vietnamese daughter. He questioned all the neighbors and even called the Montreal and Toronto police departments when the news revealed that my dad was in Canada. When Martin's hope dwindled, he tucked away Mom's birthday present, which had been waiting for her after school that day.

"She should've thought about that before running away with Peter. Get up, Lon. You have to go," Agnes commanded. She made her way around Martin and glared down at my mother.

"Please, Mom, I'm sorry. Where am I supposed to go? Please!" Mom begged. She got to her feet, crying now. I started crying, too.

"Get the fuck out of my house."

Her animosity sent a jolt down my spine, and I ran to take Mom's hand. We walked out, away from the chaos and into the snowstorm. Mom wiped the wet snow off the duffel bag, and we got back into the car. We sat there as she sobbed into the steering wheel like it was the only thing in this universe that could console her. I sat frozen in the passenger seat as the howling wind wept with us. Then, after a few more sniffles, a long sigh sobered her up, and we pulled out onto the street.

"I'm hungry, Mommy," I said after a few minutes of driving.

"We'll eat when we get home."

"Where are we going?"

"Back to your dad's."

Outside, a snowy kaleidoscope obstructed the world.

2

A constant beeping nudged me to consciousness, and fluorescent lights peeled my eyelids open. I was dressed in a hospital gown, and my favorite sweater lay on a chair near my bed. Its neon pink bow dangled by its last thread.

"Don't worry, sweetheart, your mom's right here," a nurse with a Boston accent said. She pushed aside the curtain, revealing Mom. Her side of the hospital emergency room was a mess. She lay in a stretcher, and dried blood plastered her bangs to her forehead.

"Hi, baby. You're okay," Mom said with a weak smile. "We got in a car accident. Everything's okay, though. I'm okay."

The snowstorm had just begun when we left Agnes and Martin's house. The roads weren't plowed yet and were already slippery before we got on the highway. Mom was upset but tried to focus, driving slowly through the whiteout. Less than a half hour later, she lost control of the car and totaled it against the rail grade. Later, Mom told me that I kept on telling her there were creatures jumping out toward the car. At first, my silly imagination shifted her mood. Then it seemed like it became more of a distraction. Our crash happened when I kept insisting there were animals and monsters appearing out of nowhere. I have no memory of the accident. When the ambulance and fire department arrived, Mom was carried away on a stretcher and had to wait a while before they were able to pry me out from under the glove compartment.

"You're both okay. You guys are lucky," the nurse said as she pushed my stretcher closer to Mom's. I rolled onto my side so I could see Mom clearly. I pulled the scratchy white sheet higher over me. I watched as the nurses came and went, checking on her and cleaning off her face. They gave me crackers and juice, which settled my grumbling stomach.

Finally, the doctor was ready to discharge us.

"It looks like you have a scalp laceration, but no other injuries," he said. "The nurses will help you get dressed so you can go home. Over-the-counter Tylenol and ibuprofen should be enough for the pain, but I'll write you a script in case you need something more." He looked up from his chart. "Is there someone you can call to pick you up?"

"Yeah." Mom nodded.

He closed his chart and tucked it under his armpit. "Listen, you guys got really lucky. Does your daughter have a car seat?"

"A what?" Mom asked, sitting up a bit.

"A car seat. She shouldn't be riding in the passenger seat like that. The seat belt is too big for toddlers. It took a long time for the fire department to extract her from inside the car. She needs a car seat," he emphasized.

"Okay. I'll get one," Mom agreed despite not quite under-standing the English term and how it differed from the passenger seat I was in.

"Okay, then. If you don't have any questions, then I'll let you be on your way. Be safe." With that, the doctor turned to leave as the nurse slipped back into the room.

"Thank you, Doctor," Mom said.

"If you press '9' before the number, you can make an outside call," the nurse said, unraveling the telephone cord and placing the receiver on the stretcher next to Mom. "I'll be right back with your discharge instructions."

Mom picked up the phone, dialed a number, and hung up before it had time to ring.

The nurse returned a few minutes later. "Okay, here's all your paperwork and a prescription for pain medication if you need it. Let me take your IV out, and then you guys can get dressed," the nurse said. "Do you have any questions?"

"No. Thank you," Mom said.

We gathered our belongings. Mom picked up her duffel bag, and I balled up my tattered sweater so Mom could fix it later. "I'll sew it when we get home," she said when she noticed the pink and white fabric in my hands.

We walked out to the waiting room and took a seat by the exit. Mom shuffled a few things around in the duffel bag to find the Nokia cell phone. She dialed and closed her eyes. "Hello. It's me," she said and held her breath.

All I could hear was the hostility of Dad's voice trying to strangle her from the other end.

"We're at New England Hospital. We got in a car accident.

The car's wrecked," Mom said when Dad finally stopped shouting. She nodded a few times and then hung up. We walked out through the emergency department's automatic sliding doors, and a burst of cold air made me shiver. We approached the taxi parked on the corner.

The driver rolled down his window.

"Need a cab?" His breath was visible in the icy air.

"Can you please take us to Methuen?"

"North past the city? It's gonna take a long time to get there in this weather, lady. You sure you wanna make the trip tonight?"

"That's okay. We're in no rush."

"All right, hop on in, then," he said before rolling up his window.

I got in, rested my feet on the duffel bag, and leaned my head against Mom. Her arm braced me as the cold metal seat belt buckles lay loose on the other side of the back seat.

3

The snow wasn't bad back home. By the time we got through Boston, the roads had been plowed and there were chunks of salt littering the sidewalks. Mom handed the driver a bill from her duffel bag. Dad was already opening the front door before we were even out of the taxi. He came outside in a white T-shirt.

"Hey, Daddy." I gave him a hug with one arm as I held on to my sweater with my other.

"Hey, baby. Get inside quick. It's cold. I don't want you getting sick," he said.

I ran into the house, dragging my wet boots on the rug. I turned around to watch Mom and Dad through the storm door as they stood outside.

As soon as the taxi drove off, Dad grabbed Mom by the hair. He pulled her face to his and berated her. "Where the fuck did you think you were going? You fucking ungrateful slut!" His other hand clutched her throat. "Where the fuck did you think you were going with my money and my daughter? You thought you were going somewhere, huh? You're not fucking going anywhere!" He shoved her to the ground.

"Mom!" I ran outside, shaking as if I suddenly realized it was freezing.

"Ting-Ting, get back in the house," Dad snapped. I could see the heat rising from his skin in the cold air. I stepped back.

Mom slowly got up, and he shoved her back down to the ground. "Give me my fucking money." He ripped the duffel from her shoulder. Mom tried to get up again. He pushed her harder into the cement walkway and kicked her in the ribs.

"Stop it, Daddy!" I cried, but he couldn't hear me through his fury. Mom was in a fetal position moaning as I kept screaming, afraid to get any closer.

One by one, the lights turned on in the neighbors' windows. Minutes later, sirens and flashing lights turned onto our street. "Get up, bitch. Come on!" Dad backed away from her, his arms folded across his chest as the police car parked in front of them.

Mom got to her feet, holding her sides, and two police officers stepped out of the car.

"Good evening," one of the cops said. "We got a call about a disturbance out here. Can you tell me what's going on?"

"Nothing, Officer. My wife and daughter just got home from the hospital. They got in a bad accident earlier tonight," Dad said.

"Is that your daughter over there?" The cop nodded in my direction.

"Yeah, that's her."

"She seems pretty upset," the officer said.

"Yeah, she is. She's still shaken up over the car accident. The car was completely wrecked."

"Are you okay, ma'am?" The police officer shifted his attention to Mom.

With her head still down, she nodded yes.

"Ma'am, is there anything you would like to tell us?" he asked, bending down slightly to her level.

No reply.

"The neighbors called because they were worried that someone was being hurt. Are you okay?" he asked again.

She lifted her head. "Yes, Officer, I'm fine."

"You don't look okay," he said.

"Like I said, Officer, they got into a bad car accident. No major injuries, though. Just a few bumps and scratches," Dad said. "Lucky, huh?"

"I wasn't talking to you." The cop didn't take his eyes off Mom. "Do you and your daughter feel safe here tonight?"

"Yes, Officer," Mom said. "We're fine."

"Okay, then," the cop said, shaking his head.

The two officers retreated to their cruiser.

"Try to keep it down. It's late," the second police officer said before getting into the passenger side. We all watched until the cop car was out of sight.

"Let's go inside," Dad said. His hand on my shoulder guided my body into the house. "What about Mommy?" My head rotated in her direction. She hadn't moved.

"She's coming. Get cleaned up for bed, okay?"

I took off my wet socks and pants and crawled into bed.

I tucked my ruined sweater under my pillow and stared into the shadows.

I heard Mom enter and the storm door shut behind her.

"You do something like that again, Lon, I'll kill you."

INTERLUDE

L on was stunning, with lavish black waves of hair cascading down to her shoulders and skin like untouched pearls. Trung had to have her the moment he saw her arrive at the college party. She was still in high school but had snuck out of the house to meet her best friend, Lynn, and Lynn's older sister, Amy, who had driven them to Boston. When Trung approached Lon, the spark between them was undeniable.

Trung was handsome. He had a defined jawline and a playful smile that perked up his squared-off cheekbones. With less than a dozen words, he could charm an entire room of people. He was clean-cut and had a crisp sense of fashion. You could often find him in an impeccable fitted suit, platinum cufflinks, and polished leather shoes.

They were inseparable for the rest of the night and talked for hours. They learned that they had a great deal in common, from living through the Vietnam War to the Malaysian refugee camp to their first sight of Boston's city lights. When it was time to go, Trung knew he had to see her again.

"Who was that?" Lynn asked after he'd left. She elbowed Lon, who blushed. "He's totally obsessed with you!"

"You think so?" Lon asked.

"He didn't pay anyone else no mind as soon as he met you," Amy confirmed. She already knew Trung, as they had mutual friends in Boston's Vietnamese community. Rumor had it that he was a gangster, but he claimed to be in the restaurant business. "And Trung is an outgoing guy. He's usually talking to everyone. He's definitely into you."

"We'll see. I'm not so sure he's that interested." Despite her words, Lon was smitten. Inside, she hoped that the girls were right.

One spring day a week after Lon and Trung first met, Lon saw his Mercedes pull up outside. She ran to the stairs, sat down on the top step, and waited for the doorbell. Agnes answered it.

"Hi, Mrs. Schafer," Trung said with his dapper smile. "You look lovely as usual. Is Lon home by any chance?" He held up a bouquet of red roses and tiger lilies. It was the third time Trung had stopped by since the college party. The first time, he had dropped off a bracelet. The second time, it was a mink coat.

"She's upstairs doing her homework," Agnes said, folding her arms across her chest.

"I don't mind waiting until she's done." Trung peered around the door.

"Today is not a good day, Peter. Maybe another time. I'll give her the flowers." He handed them over and Agnes sniffed the flowers. "They're beautiful."

"Okay. I'll come by another day. Will you tell her I stopped by?"

Lon squealed and raced back to her window in her room to watch him go. She lifted it open and waved. "Thanks for the flowers!" she said in Vietnamese.

Trung blew her a kiss before driving off.

Trung continued to drop by with gifts for Lon—and, eventually, gifts for Agnes and Martin as well. When he tried to give them an extravagant painting during one visit, they wouldn't accept it and began to wonder how Trung was affording these luxuries on a restaurant employee's salary. But Trung's perseverance led Agnes and Martin to discuss the possibility of allowing Lon to see him.

Their age difference was the biggest concern. Lon was fourteen and Trung was twenty-two, which was inappropriate by American standards. However, in Vietnamese culture, it was quite normal for women to date and marry men much older than themselves. On the other hand, because they lived in a predominantly White neighborhood, they didn't want to deprive Lon of the few friends she had from her own ethnic background. They were afraid that it would impinge on her sense of belonging as an immigrant in the United States.

So, one day, when Trung rang the doorbell and politely asked to see Lon, Agnes and Martin invited him inside. They sat down at the dining room table, and Martin set the boundaries. Trung was permitted to spend time with Lon, as long as it was limited and they stayed within the town of Hingham, where they lived.

Lon and Trung eagerly agreed and went on their first impromptu date. They walked two blocks down the road to a small beach and watched the tide drift out as they got to know each other.

"How is it living with that family?" Trung asked.

"It's okay. They're really nice to me."

"Yeah, but they're so different," he pointed out.

Lon had to agree. They were Christian, conservative, opinionated, and raised in a country of privilege and comfort. Everything from the food they ate to the music they played was different.

"Don't you miss your culture?" Trung asked. "Your people?"

Of course Lon did, but she'd had no control over the events that brought her here. She had to remember to be grateful for her adoption; dwelling on the rest only broke her heart.

"Well, at least you have me now." Trung wrapped his arm around her shoulder.

Lon sat in a clinic lobby across from another girl similar in age. The girl was accompanied by her mother. They sat there without saying much, their arms linked, waiting to be called.

For the last two weeks, Lon had been stricken with nausea and fatigue. She was repelled by food and had trouble keeping her eyes open during class. When she told her best friend, Lynn, about her symptoms, she suggested that Lon take a pregnancy test.

Two pink lines popped up on the stick, and Lon was inundated with shame as she stared at the results. The thought of carrying a baby during high school was mortifying, and there was no way she would subject herself to that embarrassment. Between being an immigrant, speaking broken English, and her dislike for academics, high school was hard enough.

She made an appointment at an abortion clinic a few towns over that Lynn had told her about. But as soon as she arrived, it felt wrong. The dilemma weighed on her like a barbell that she didn't have the strength to force off her chest. After a few minutes of waiting, she left.

She called Trung as soon as she could. "Can you meet me at the beach? I have to tell you something important."

When Trung arrived, the waves were crashing and Lon was sitting by the shore, fiddling with the sand. He sat down close to her. Lon continued to gaze out at the water.

"I'm pregnant," she said, her eyes welling up.

Trung pulled her close and held her as they listened to the ocean.

"What are you going to do?" he finally asked.

"I want to have the baby," Lon said.

"Okay."

"But I can't tell Agnes and Martin. They're very religious, and they believe sex before marriage is a sin. And I don't want to be a pregnant girl at Hingham High. I just can't. I would be a disgrace. I don't know what to do." She started to panic.

"Shh, shh, shh. It's okay, Lon. Don't worry about any of that. You can have the baby. *We* will have *our* baby." He looked deep into her eyes. "Everything's going to be okay," Trung promised.

Before the sun had bid farewell to the day, Lon and Trung had devised a plan. On Lon's birthday, she would put what she needed in her backpack and go to school like normal. But instead of getting on the bus to go home afterward, she would start walking home. Trung would pick her up at the stop sign not far down the street. They would run away, start a family, and raise the baby together.

"I'll take care of you, Lon." Trung caressed her face. "I'll take care of everything. I love you."

4

The love story that led to my existence would be nothing more than an unfinished fairy tale. I rewrote the next chapter in my mind over and over again throughout my childhood and as an adult, but the ending remained a letdown. I do not have a single positive memory of their relationship, and my earliest memory is that harrowing night we tried to leave Dad. Any attempt I have made at romanticizing their affair fails like a candle lit on a windy day. Mom didn't run away with Dad to find intimacy and unconditional support. I wasn't the blessing that kept them together and helped them grow. In fact, Dad never even married her.

I was born on May 7, 1985, at Bon Secours Hospital in Methuen, Massachusetts, as Felicia Truong, my American name—Ting-Ting was my given Chinese name. I wasn't given a Vietnamese name because although Dad was from Vietnam, he was ethnically Chinese. It's not uncommon for Asian immigrants to take up English names to assimilate into

Western culture and make it easier for Americans to pro-nounce our names. The adjustment was one way to fit in and avoid marginalization—a survival tactic. However, what was uncommon was the first name Mom chose for me. While pregnant with me, she was watching a movie that starred a pretty and kindhearted Spanish princess by the name of Felicia, and the character resonated with her. In Latin, the meaning of Felicia is happiness. In another version of Mom and Dad's fairy tale, I fantasized that I eventually became the happily ever after for her.

My mother is Loan Anh Thai and her American name is Jennifer. After being adopted by the Schafers, they continued to address her as Loan, which evolved into Lon, but outside of the home, she introduced herself as Jennifer. She resided with the Schafers for about a year before running off with Dad. Almost immediately afterward, it was obvious that he was not the restaurant manager or chef he claimed to be. They couldn't walk one block in Boston without someone recognizing Dad. There was always a sense of intimidation when people inter-acted with him and an overzealous urge to please him. He wore Mom on his arm like a flashy Rolex and showed her off, making sure that everyone knew she was strictly his. When he left for hours and came back with piles of cash, she didn't ask questions. Then when he started to carry a handgun when they went out, Mom acted as if she didn't notice. In these brief honeymoon months after he saved her from a culturally foreign world, she trusted Dad with her life. Mom was in love.

My dad's full name is Trung Chi Truong, his nickname is Ah Sing, and his American name is Peter. Although he is ethnically

Chinese, he immigrated from Vietnam during the Vietnam War and landed on Texan soil. By 1980, Dad had moved to Boston, where he was introduced to the realm of organized crime.

He started out by doing dirty work for the gang leaders of Boston's Chinatown. Chinatown was located in the southern part of the city. A *paifang*, a traditional Chinese architectural arch on Beach Street, decorated with gold Chinese calligraphy and a roof covered in green tiles, was the gateway into the nine-block area. During Dad's era, there was a consistent and major increase in Chinatown's population after the Chinese Exclusion Act was abolished in 1943. Asian immigrants, especially Chinese and Vietnamese, settled in this neighborhood to take advantage of its low-cost housing and job opportunities. Gradually, it transformed into a community where immigrant families could retain a sense of identity and support one another as they struggled to thrive. The adversity associated with immigration and the pressure to develop in challenging and unfamiliar circumstances not only bred hardworking, law-abiding newcomers but also those who resorted to delinquency in order to sustain themselves.

Dad got involved with Stephen Tse, head of the Ping On triad, which was a gang that ran organized crime in Chinatown. At first, this involved collecting extortion money from local stores and making various deliveries, but it wasn't long before Dad was sanctioning armed robberies and execution hits on gang rivals. He quickly gained power and became one of Tse's chief lieutenants. This transition happened around the time he met Mom.

But Dad didn't stop there.

He was reckless and impulsive, and the heists he ran with the gang were some of the bloodiest scenes that officers had ever witnessed. When he went rogue and ordered freelance robberies in and around Boston, Tse banned Dad's association with Ping On. Despite Ping On's control of gambling operations, loan-sharking, prostitution, and drug trafficking, with Tse in charge, the streets were largely free of violence. Dad was unpredictable and aggressive, attracting too much unwanted attention from the police. Tse knew he had to detach his syndicate from the heat.

When Tse cut ties with him, Dad went on to recruit his own gang of Vietnamese immigrants arriving in Boston. The Vietnamese population was growing exponentially as a result of the country's communist takeover and continued war in Southeast Asia. Many young Vietnamese men joined gangs for protection and a sense of belonging. Others created gangs of their own. In the mid-1980s, Dad formed Ah Sing's Boys. At the same time, Tse was jailed, and his influence rapidly slipped. The collision of these events initiated the most heinous era of violence in Chinatown history. The sudden upsurge in gang presence led to feuds over territory and rivalries vying for power. Gang warfare erupted, and Dad's tactics were dominating. An investigator once commented in a *Boston Globe* article, "He was the most dangerous Vietnamese gangbanger in North America. You just say his name and everybody runs."[1]

---

1   Anne E. Kornblut, "Guilty Plea Ends Gang Terror Spree," *Boston Globe*, January 13, 1998, B5.

5

On the opposite side of the shatterproof glass, Dad appeared, dressed in a faded orange jumpsuit. He sat down and picked up the phone that connected to another phone that Mom already had pressed to her ear. I shared a chair with Mom, fidgeting to make room for us both as I awaited my turn to talk to him. Without a phone of my own, his voice sounded muffled to me. I couldn't understand what he was saying, but I could see the tension in his eyebrows. Dad did most of the talking while Mom acknowledged everything he said with a nod or an "Mm-hmm."

I didn't understand what was happening at the time, but in June 1988, less than six months after our car accident, Dad was convicted for armed robbery and received an eighteen-year sentence. In November, he was transferred to the Massachusetts Correctional Institute in Shirley. He had been inside for twelve days when Mom and I visited him there.

When they were done, Mom hoisted me into her lap so I could reach the phone. I pushed my fingertips against the glass until my nail beds blanched inside his palm. My small toddler hand could disappear into his. If I tried hard enough, maybe I could feel his bare skin before we had to leave.

"What's up, baby?" Dad's mood relaxed.

"Nothing. What are you doing here?"

"Visiting, baby. You don't have to worry about anything."

"Okay." I believed him.

"Look at you, looking more and more like your daddy every day." He grinned. "You know what that means?"

"What?" I cocked my head to the side.

"It means you're a beautiful little girl, the next Miss Chinatown."

He called me that all the time. He carried me around Kneeland Street, telling anyone who would listen that I was the future Miss Chinatown. Miss Chinatown USA was a pageant held during Lunar New Year celebrations. It was an alternative pageant created for Chinese American women when qualified candidates weren't allowed to enter Miss America because they were not members of the White race. Of course, everyone agreed with him. They had to agree because everyone knew Dad was a loose cannon. If you didn't tell him I was the prettiest girl you had ever seen, you could be risking your life.

"Do you look like your mommy?" he asked with a skeptical smirk.

I looked back and scanned her features, examining her lovely round face, short forehead, and cupid lips. I giggled. "No, I look like you."

"What looks like your daddy's?" he prompted.

"My nose." I pointed at his through the glass.

"And?"

"My eyes."

"And?"

"My chin." I pointed at mine. I couldn't touch his.

"And?"

I tapped my forehead. "Everything!" We used to play out this lighthearted exchange for his amusement.

"That's right," Dad laughed. "I love you, baby. Now let me talk to your mommy again." I passed the phone back to her and hopped off her lap. A few minutes later, we waved goodbye as the security guard unlocked the gate, slid the bars open, and let Dad through. I looked beyond him as he marched down a dull hallway.

When we got back to the apartment, Mom was quiet. She paced from room to room, scanning them all with anxious eyes yet never seeming to find what she was looking for. When she reached the kitchen, she paused and started fixing me a bowl of chicken with rice and soy sauce. She sat with me at the table, no meal of her own, and picked at her cuticles. Distracted by her thoughts, she waited for me to finish eating. Afterward, she cleaned up.

She couldn't stay static that evening. Constantly on the move, Mom organized papers and then folded clothes, gathered some belongings, and eventually packed them. I fell asleep as she kept busy. In the middle of the night, I awoke and noticed her in bed with me. She was in a peaceful slumber, nestled up close to me under my pink and purple blanket. I glanced over at her bed. It was made up neatly, with two closed suitcases sitting on top.

We woke up to a bright, late-autumn day and headed to my Uncle Vincent's house, which was a twenty-minute drive away, while it was still early.

Vincent was Dad's younger brother and closest sibling. They were the first two members of their family to leave Saigon during the Vietnam War. Together, they took a four-day boat ride from Vietnam to a Malaysian refugee camp, where they spent eleven months before arriving in America. My uncle earned his citizenship and started a hair salon business in Boston while my father was entering the criminal underworld. I think Uncle Vincent was the only family member who respected Mom or at least treated her like a human being. He spoke to her in Vietnamese, mindful that this was Mom's native tongue, as everyone else spoke in Cantonese, a dialect of the Chinese language. Dad's entire family was fluently bilingual in Cantonese and Vietnamese. However, Cantonese was the predominant language spoken around me when I was growing up, and no one bothered to accommodate Mom. Instead, they talked around her. Occasionally, they paused and glanced her way, curious if she understood their conversation, and then continued in Cantonese.

We spent the entire day at his house with my grandparents and my aunt. Aunt Grace, a delicate woman sick with Lupus, was one of my dad's older sisters. She had a butterfly-shaped rash across her rosy cheeks, which were always puffy from the steroids she took to manage her illness.

Suddenly, we heard a commotion coming from the front door. Mom and I were lounging in the living room, and we shot up from the sofa. Dad barged through the door and sprinted up the foyer stairs.

"Daddy?" I gasped. Everyone else seemed to be expecting his arrival.

He picked me up for a quick hug and then asked the gathered adults, "Where's Vincent?"

Maa-Maa pointed down the hallway. Dad lowered me to the floor and walked straight into Uncle Vincent's bedroom without a knock.

A heated discussion erupted behind closed doors. The rest of us remained sitting in the living room. No one looked at each other. We listened to Dad and Uncle Vincent quarrel and then calm down.

Uncle Vincent emerged from the bedroom. He had changed into black slacks and a T-shirt that read, "LeGala Salon," and was in a rush to meet his first client of the day.

"You should have everything you need. Stay safe, brother. Call if you need anything," he said, slapping Dad on the back before heading out the door.

"Ready, Lon?" Dad asked Mom. "Come on, go get your stuff."

He ignored Maa-Maa and Yeh-Yeh.

"You need to grow up," Yeh-Yeh said. "You have a wife and daughter now. You run, and then what? What's your plan?"

"I have a plan," Dad said. "Don't worry about me."

"You have to think. Use your head, stupid," he scolded, tapping the back of Dad's head. "You can't run forever. You need to settle down. Be a man and take care of your family." Yeh-Yeh shook his head in disgust.

Mom got up, and I started to follow. Maa-Maa gently grabbed my arm, but I wiggled away.

"You're going to stay here tonight, Ting-Ting. Daddy and I will be back soon," Mom said and then looked away.

"I want to go with you guys, though," I whined.

Mom looked at Dad for permission. I looked at him for it, too. For a moment, there was contemplation in his eyes. Then, he shook his head.

"It's too dangerous," he said.

"You have to stay here so you can start preschool. Remember how excited you are for school? If you come with us, you might miss it. I promise you, baby, we'll be back soon," Mom said.

"I'll start school later, Mommy. I wanna go with you and Dad."

She pulled me close, and warm tears absorbed into my shirt.

"We gotta go, Lon," Dad urged.

Maa-Maa, Yeh-Yeh, and I walked them out. One of the suitcases we'd brought stayed in the house. The second suitcase was loaded into the trunk of Dad's car.

"I love you so much. You be a good girl, okay? We'll be back soon," Mom said through her open passenger window.

I followed them to the foot of the driveway, hoping they would change their minds, open the rear door, and tell me to get in. That didn't happen. The car reversed onto the street. I refrained from chasing them as I watched them disappear beyond the corner.

From there, they drove north without stopping. Dad had just escaped from the Massachusetts Correctional Institute—just thirteen days after his conviction and one day after we visited him. Hours later, my parents crossed the Canadian border. By leaving the country, they kicked off a tireless international manhunt by the authorities.

6

Months passed, seasons changed, and the amber tinge of summer seeped into the edges of maple leaves. It was autumn again, and I was scheduled to start prekindergarten. Mom called every day. Sometimes we talked; sometimes I missed her calls. During every call, she told me that they were coming for me soon. How soon? She couldn't give me an answer. My enthusiasm for the start of school tapered, and anxiety set in.

On the first day of class, I stood on the front steps, waiting for the school bus with a brand-new backpack filled with sharp Lisa Frank pencils and a blank notebook.

I spent the entire first day mute. I sat alone in the cafeteria. I skipped recess. I listened. I learned. I went home and read my books as my grandparents tuned in to the nightly news. It took a week to get used to it, but by the second week, I found myself enjoying my days: the schedule, the subjects, the stability.

I don't remember interacting with Maa-Maa and Yeh-Yeh very much. They were probably in their late fifties and not used to being full-time caretakers to a child born in the United States. I learned more Cantonese while living with them and studied English at school. Maa-Maa resented Mom and didn't approve of Dad being with a woman outside of their ethnicity. I think some of the friction rubbed off on me. She was taking care of me for my dad and made it clear she wasn't doing Mom any favors. I felt more like a chore to her than a granddaughter, and because of that, at four years old, I became self-sufficient and required minimal supervision. I washed up, got dressed, and fed and cleaned up after myself. I was obedient and never asked Maa-Maa or Yeh-Yeh for a thing. Yeh-Yeh was quiet, but out of the two, something told me that he cared about me. Maybe it was the tone he used when I overheard him reprimanding my parents for not being there for me, as if I deserved more, or maybe because every time he peeled an orange, he split it and always handed me the bigger half. Yeh-Yeh made me feel safe.

One day during my second week of school, Mr. Nardone, my teacher, turned us loose for recess, as usual. "Try not to run 'til you get outside," he hollered as the other students rushed out the door to the playground. "Have fun. See you guys in a bit."

As the last kid exited, he returned to his desk by the chalkboard. Seeing me still at my desk, he asked, "Not going out to recess today either, huh?" He was a short man with brown olive-tinged skin and a droopy nose.

I shook my head no. I still hadn't participated in recess, even though I was growing used to everything else about school.

"It's a beautiful day out there." He glanced toward the windows. I looked as well. A brilliant sun pierced the pale blue sky. "You sure you don't want to join the rest?" he asked as he slid his glasses down to the base of his nose.

"I'm sure," I said, smiling.

"Okay. Let me know if you change your mind," he said as he picked up a stack of papers, placed them in front of him, and uncapped his red marker.

I sat there for thirty minutes organizing my desk, examining the classroom posters, and observing Mr. Nardone until recess was over. He was perhaps the only person I had talked to after my parents left. I didn't interact with the other students, and my grandparents mainly kept to themselves. But during our shared recess together, Mr. Nardone would awkwardly inform me whenever he had to leave the classroom, whether it was to use the restroom or grab a soda. When he grew tired of his papers, he would take off his glasses and ask me random questions.

"So, what's your favorite color?" he asked me one day.

"Pink."

"Oh. Okay. That's a nice color."

He leaned back in his chair and twirled a pen between his fingers.

"Do you know what you want to be when you grow up?" he asked.

"A pediatrician."

"Wow, that's great! I think you could probably be one," he said before turning back to his papers.

I was proud of my answer. I had heard the term *pediatrician* during a program on the nightly news my grandparents watched. I took his response as a compliment. Despite whatever he thought of my refusal to go to recess, I had big plans for myself.

By the third week of school, Mr. Nardone had started to take more interest in my decision to sit out recess.

"Do you want to go out with the other kids today?" he asked one day as he approached my desk. I shrugged. "Come on. Let's go together," he said, holding on to the back of my chair.

We walked outside. In front of us was a concrete basketball court. There was a jungle gym to the left and a swing set to the right. Standing at Mr. Nardone's side, I watched everyone play for the entire period. We didn't say a word. A few girls were picking dandelions and tucking them behind their ears and into their braids. A student sprinted past me as he chased another boy in a game of tag. Legs pumped as the swings launched higher and higher. Laughter and loud voices bounced through the air. It all felt strange to me. When recess was over, we went back inside to finish the school day.

The next day, when the other children went outside for recess, Mr. Nardone set aside his pile of papers and offered to go outside with me again. I politely declined and went back to sharpening my pencils. The idea of engaging in fun with the other children made me feel uncomfortable—an emotion that a therapist would later tell me was triggered by trauma. Inside of my child-sized body, my heart and brain matured against my will. I was forced to grow up before I was given a chance to be a kid. I worried about things that other children had the luxury of taking for granted. I was visiting Dad in prison while they watched Saturday morning cartoons, or tucking myself into bed after a phone call with parents I had not seen in almost a year as they listened to bedtime stories and hugged their teddy bears. The isolation was not intentional. It was the natural consequence of being deprived of a true childhood. There was nothing out there for me. Not my dad and not my mom. Anyway, I preferred learning over playing. The alphabet gave me a sense of order, and math was reliable. That was what I needed.

Every day, as soon as we slowed to turn onto my street, I squinted through the bus window to get a glimpse of the driveway, hoping a black Mercedes would be parked there, with Mom and Dad leaning on the trunk, awaiting my arrival.

The time my parents were gone felt like a lifetime. It was about a year, though. Mom later told me that they were only gone for months and definitely less than a year. Late one evening between fall and winter, I was in the guest room looking for some paper to write on when the door swung open. I turned around, and Mom was standing there, glowing. Astonished, I jumped into her arms so hard that I almost knocked her over. I clutched her, afraid that if I let up even a tiny bit, I would lose her again.

"Oh, my goodness, I'm so happy to see you!" She swayed me from side to side for a moment and then put me down to look at me. When our eyes met, I suddenly began to cry. At the time, I wasn't sure why, because I was filled with joy. This flood of tears, which I had been holding in since the day they left, broke the dam. And although I was happy to see Mom, I was so mad and hurt. She had left me abruptly and couldn't tell me when she was coming back. And every day that she didn't return, I became more and more scared that she never would. She missed my first day of school, my first school bus pickup, my first step toward success.

"Oh, no, don't cry. I'm here now. Don't cry, baby. It's okay." She wiped my eyes. "We're back, and I won't ever leave you again."

In the midst of my elation, I hadn't been aware that someone was with Mom. Now, I noticed on the floor beside us was a small chubby baby in green footy pajamas. With her plump cheeks and big brown eyes, she stared up at me from her car seat. Mom held my hand, lightly pulled me toward her, and rocked the baby back and forth.

"This is your baby sister, Yeem Kwon," she said. I touched the bottom of her foot. I didn't think much of her besides that she was kind of cute. Born in Montreal, Canada, she was given the American name Amanda and was only just a newborn. The fact that my sister had a car seat when I hadn't came down to a couple of things. By this time, Mom had been living among Western culture for over five years. She had become more proficient in English and had adapted to social norms, so she no longer had the same confusion about what a car seat was. Furthermore, Mom and Dad wanted to be prepared to cross the border without any other reason to be stopped. I tried not to take it personally.

We packed my stuff, said goodbye to my grandparents, and went to our new home, a furnished one-bedroom townhouse on the outskirts of Boston with a loft and a backyard.

"I told you that I was going to take care of you guys," Dad said as he threw the keys onto the dining table and kicked off his shoes. "You like it?"

He laughed as I ran from room to room. We hadn't lived in a place this nice in a while. Our previous home was older, with faded floors and bent-up blinds. I didn't notice many details of each residence since we had been accustomed to leaving within the year or less before we could fully settle in. We never hung picture frames, filled all of the cabinets, or needed magnets for the refrigerator.

Unlike our previous homes, it seemed modern. The paint on the walls was fresh and spotless. The carpet wasn't broken in and the ceilings were tall. "I love it! Is this my room up here?" I shouted from the loft.

"Yes, baby," Mom responded. She unfastened Amanda and went to the kitchen. I had the entire upper level to myself. It was even equipped with a TV and a CD player. Dad went out to the patio and lit up a Marlboro Red. We were together. No one fought. It was the happiest night of my life.

7

Things seemed to be better. Dad had been on the run since escaping the low security prison in Shirley, Massachusetts. In addition to the townhouse, we also had another apartment nearby and condos in Montreal and Toronto, so Dad had a place to stay as he remained mobile.

Mom was occupied with the baby and didn't mind him being away as much as she did before they went to Canada. With all the inconsistency, I didn't enroll in school again. We were far enough away that I wasn't able to attend the same prekindergarten. I wouldn't sit in another classroom until next fall when actual kindergarten started. I was intentionally acquiescent and reserved to minimize any stress in our home. I helped Mom with Amanda and continued to become more and more independent.

Between the racketeering, robberies, and extortion, Dad was bringing in tens of thousands of dollars per week. Despite this cash flow—and his willingness to spend it on housing—Dad didn't give Mom much money. In fact, he encouraged her to find a job and let her drive a run-down Honda Accord while he rode around in a shiny Mercedes-Benz. With each visit home, he gave Mom a few hundred dollars, which was barely enough to cover gas, diapers, bills, and groceries.

To this day, Mom's explanation for this was that he was "a piece of shit. He didn't love us, that's why." To an extent, I believed this to be the clearest rationale, but there seemed to be more complexity underlying his reason for not providing for us. It was a form of manipulation. Money was a necessity, and he knew it was nearly impossible for Mom to support us on her own. So he gave her cash when we were on the brink of nothing, too desperate to reject the finances, however insignificant the amount, and often enough that we relied on him. On the other end of his exploitation, this was a demonstration of the power and control Dad had over us. He had an obsession with power, and he showed us how dire our situation could be at his disposal. On account of this, Mom was forced to apply for welfare, and we started collecting food stamps.

One day, as we stood in the checkout line at the grocery store, Mom counted out the red, blue, and purple paper bills and handed them over to the cashier.

"I'm sorry, ma'am, but this doesn't pay for the diapers or the toilet paper." The cashier tapped the key on the register, chomped her bubblegum, and scrolled through the receipt. "Oh, and it doesn't cover the candy bar, either." She looked at Mom. Mom looked at me, and we put those items back.

The federal investigation into Dad's whereabouts was escalating along with the rise in gang activity in Boston, Toronto, and Montreal. He had remained active during my stay with

Maa-Maa and Yeh-Yeh while he and Mom were in Canada. He became known as the *dai lo*, Cantonese for elder brother and slang for head boss, of an intensely loyal Vietnamese street gang. The gang consisted of an estimated forty to sixty men who oversaw organized crime. A wave of unprecedented violent robberies of Toronto's and Montreal's Chinatown stores took place, and underground gambling dens began appearing in both cities. Ten people were found dead in Toronto, all of whom were associates of Dad's main rival. In Boston, his gang was behind a triple murder inside of a restaurant. A Boston police detective who had met Dad in Massachusetts described him as "a vicious, vicious person," notorious for his trademark anger.[2] Newspapers were calling it the most brutal span of Asian American crime in history.[3]

As the headlines were being printed and Dad ascended to the top of the nation's most-wanted list, he came home more and more infrequently. When he did make it home to see us, he didn't spend the night. He would give me and Amanda a hug and a kiss and fifteen minutes of attention and then go off to make phone calls and answer pages, chain-smoking and pacing as the paranoia of getting captured built.

Before he left, there was always an altercation between him and Mom. Their fights were getting worse. Flashes of his rage from the night he beat Mom were resurfacing, and Dad was becoming abusive again. One night, he threw Mom against the wall and choked her when she threatened to steal his money if

2   Dan Burke and Paul Kaihla, "Inside the Gangs: An Underworld Reign of Terror," *Maclean's*, March 25, 1991, 22.

3   Anne E. Kornblut, "Guilty Plea Ends Gang Terror Spree," *Boston Globe*, January 13, 1998, B5.

he didn't start providing for us. During a different argument, Dad shoved her down a flight of stairs after she told him that she would leave him for someone else if he didn't start acting like a man.

Inevitably, a day or so later, Dad would call and apologize for striking her. "You know I love you, Lon. I messed up. It won't happen again." He always swore he would make it up to her, and the next time he would come home, Mom would let him in.

I hated the fights. Not because I was scared—I knew Dad wouldn't hurt me or Amanda—but because it was confusing. I watched Dad use violence and verbal abuse against Mom and then watched her subject herself to his torture despite how painful it all was. Then I heard them tell each other, "I love you," and claim that they loved us too. Their fights made me feel disappointed, not only in them for doing this again but also in us as a family.

One evening when Dad decided to show up, I asked if he could spend the night and watch *The Little Mermaid* with me and Amanda. I was almost six years old and already outgrowing princess movies, but it was Amanda's favorite.

"You wanna watch *The Little Mermaid*? Go ahead and put it on. Daddy will watch it with you," he said, sitting down on the couch.

My eyes were wide with excitement. Amanda and I had been watching *The Little Mermaid* at least three times a day since she discovered it, but not once had we ever watched it with Dad. I popped the videotape into the VCR, picked Amanda up, and snuggled on the couch next to him. Before Ariel could even sing her first song, Dad stepped out to make a phone call. The second time he stepped out, he needed a cigarette. The third time, it was to make another phone call. I watched him through the glass door, his lips moving fast as he talked into his phone and paced our cement patio. Amanda lay on her side, mesmerized by Sebastian the crab and his Jamaican accent. I went to the dining room and pushed a chair up under the doorknob of the front door.

"What are you doing, Felicia?" Mom asked from the kitchen. I ignored her and moved the next chair until all six dining chairs barricaded our front door.

Dad returned to the house, went over to Amanda, and kissed her on the cheek. Her gaze was still stuck like glue to the Disney princess on the screen. "Okay, baby, I gotta go. Come give Daddy a kiss," he said, waving at me. The chairs caught his attention. "What's that?" Dad asked.

"If you leave tonight, don't come back, Daddy," I said.

"Ha! Did you put her up to this, Lon? Did your mother tell you to do this?"

"It's not funny, Trung," Mom said.

"What's so important that you can't be here with us?" I asked.

"I have to work, honey. One day you'll understand."

"I'm old enough to understand now. Is work more important than us?"

"You're five. I know you think you understand, but you don't, baby. I gotta go."

"If you walk out that door, Daddy, don't come back."

I had overheard Mom yell this multiple times at Dad in the past as he turned his back toward her to leave. The difference was that I meant it. He came and went as he pleased and saw us whenever he wanted to, but when I wanted to see Dad, I had to wait days, sometimes even weeks. It wasn't fair.

He rubbed his forehead and sighed. For a moment, I thought he would stay, put his pager on standby, unbutton his white collared shirt, and sink into the sofa between his daughters. I thought he would choose us.

My heart went heavy like an anchor drifting to the ocean floor when Dad went to the door and began putting on his shoes and tying double knots into his laces. He slowly moved one chair out of the way and maneuvered the others around me like a game of chess as I stood there in check. When he removed the last chair, I backed up against the door. Checkmate. "Are you really gonna go?" I demanded in disbelief.

"Felicia, I have to go. Daddy has to work," he said, staring at me. He bent down on one knee with his arms open gesturing for a hug. I grunted and ran upstairs.

With that, Dad took off.

By the next morning, my anger had dissipated, and all I was left with was frustration. Mom must've felt some sort of way about last night. It was the first time I had spoken out against Dad, and perhaps it was the first time she realized that he was directly hurting me too. The emotion could have been guilt or pity or sadness. I wasn't sure, but it manifested as Mom being unusually talkative. Her demeanor was more present, and her voice was gentle, as if she was trying to console me without bringing up what happened.

"We're gonna go to the plaza today so we can pick up some things," she said as she prepared our breakfast.

The plaza was a short distance away. In it was a grocery store, a bank, Sally Beauty, Dunkin' Donuts, and a few other small stores. There was also a discount store, which carried a bit of everything, including clothes, shoes, toys, home goods, and books. That was our destination this morning.

Amanda and I played hide-and-seek in the clothing racks as my mom flipped through the hangers. She picked up a cheap shirt, worked the price tag off the plastic holder, and replaced it onto a different, more expensive blouse. We checked out and went home.

"I have a job interview tomorrow. Do you think you can watch your sister?" she asked when we got home.

"Yeah." I nodded.

"Hey, I have something for you. Go grab my purse."

I handed her bag over, and she pulled out a book. I had no idea where it came from. Her expression told me to keep it our secret. My eyes lit up, and I snatched the book right out of her hands. Holding it against my chest, I smiled, silently promising not to tell anyone.

I traced my fingers over the title and fanned through the tattered pages. A whiff of stale paper brushed my face. I couldn't wait to start reading.

8

A week later, Dad came home in the middle of the night. He went straight to the bedroom and woke Mom up. I could hear them talking from my loft but couldn't make out what they were saying. I got out of bed and pressed my ear to the floor. Their bedroom was directly under my bed, but I still couldn't hear much.

Muffled by the carpet, I tiptoed down the steps and sat at the bottom of the stairs. They spoke in Vietnamese and switched to English for brief moments. Although I only understood very basic Vietnamese, between my grasp of both languages and body language, I could usually get the sense of a conversation. I couldn't hear them enough to put it all together. All I knew was that their voices were calm and remained calm throughout.

Before returning to bed, I decided to say hi to Dad and let him know I wasn't mad at him anymore. I turned the door-knob, cracked the door open slightly, and tilted my head inside, expecting to see them asleep in bed. The bed was empty.

I opened the door wider to check the other side of the bed-room. Mom and Dad were standing there utterly naked and holding each other, like a statue in a museum somewhere in Europe. They both turned their heads toward me. I shut the door in shock and sprinted upstairs.

I wrung my bedsheets and tossed my head on my pillow as I tried to comprehend their intimacy. I was haunted by the image of Mom's skin absorbing into his, her muscles at rest and her tendons lax. The futility on her face. The dominance in Dad's stance as he braced Mom's body, like a snake's jaw around a mouse before swallowing it whole. It was like a bizarre display of affection and suffering between two lost souls in a burning house.

The following day, to my surprise, Dad was in the dining room when I came down for breakfast. "Hey, baby, come give me a hug," he said.

I embraced him. I was glad that he didn't take what I'd said last week seriously.

"Sit down and eat something," he said as Mom placed two porcelain bowls on the table.

"So, listen, your mom and I were talking, and we're gonna go to Canada. All of us." He scooped up a mouthful of food with his chopsticks.

"Me too?" I asked with skepticism. "I don't have to go back to Maa-Maa and Yeh-Yeh's?"

"No, we're all going together." He squeezed my hand. "I'm going to run out for a bit now to take care of some things. You guys pack while I'm out, okay?"

I inhaled my fried eggs and rice with soy sauce and then excused myself to go get my stuff in order. I assumed this was Dad's compromise. He had to leave and work, so why not take us with him? He missed us, I bet, perhaps as much as I missed him. He knew that he'd hurt my feelings. At least he was trying.

Later, when I was an adult in my thirties, Mom told me that Dad had just been using us to look like a regular family man, as there was increasing surveillance on him. But I liked to remember that fleeting notion that I had as a child that he truly cherished me. There was a trivial part of me that indulged in the idea of having a genuine father-daughter relationship with Dad that I shooed away like a nagging housefly every time it got close. I thought of how pathetic this desire was if Dad was as coldhearted as Mom suggested. I felt ashamed for wanting love from someone who wanted nothing to do with me, who used my naivete for his own advantage. There would be a constant battle inside of me between hoping for Dad's love and rejecting any gesture of it.

"He used us, Felicia. He used us to cross into Canada. Border patrol back then wasn't what it's like now. If you had kids in the car, they let you straight through without question. We just flashed our passports and kept driving," Mom said. "He used us as an alibi. He used us in court so the jury would be more sympathetic. Peter used us for his self-interest. He didn't give a shit about us."

9

Being on the run with Dad was like going on a spontaneous, never-ending road trip. At any time of day or night, we would get in the car and go on our next unplanned adventure.

Most of our departures occurred in the middle of the night. Mom would stir me awake, with Amanda already bundled up in her other arm. "We gotta go with Daddy now," she'd whisper as I stumbled out of bed, rubbing my eyes.

In the back seat of the car, I would pass out next to my sister, and by the next day, we'd appear in a different city. We bounced around between Montreal, Toronto, New York City, Boston, and all the surrounding areas in a sporadic rotation. Sometimes, we'd stay for several days; other times, we'd be back on the highway after lunch, as soon as Dad's job was finished.

While in Canada, Dad formed another gang of forlorn Asian immigrants who were trying to earn enough money to support their families. Within two years, they were extorting ten thousand dollars a week in Montreal alone. On top of that, the armed robberies Dad organized were pulling in between one hundred thousand and five hundred thousand dollars per holdup, which were typically jewelry stores. Dad gained power as he displayed his savage intimidation tactics, unpredictable violence, and bold approach to high-yielding heists. From half a continent away, he choreographed an attack via cell phone from Montreal, commanding the robbers to reenter a store in Calgary when they started to back down. By remaining mobile and remotely enforcing his authority on over sixty gang members throughout New England and Canada, Dad solidified his presence on the most-wanted list. Law enforcement agencies became increasingly frustrated as their efforts to locate Dad and substantially link him to criminal activity proved to be ineffective.

Despite the disarray inherent in our new lifestyle as outlaws, Dad was at his peak as a father. He was present, and Mom was content. We saw him almost every day, ate meals as a family, held hands while strolling through each city's Chinatown, and spent hours together in the car. If he left, we left, which meant no worrying about food, shelter, bills, or clothes. Each transaction came home with him—and, to us—minimizing his chances of gambling it, spending it, or otherwise wasting it away before we were considered.

All of Dad's meetings were held in our apartments, too. My sister and I inherited a lot of "uncles" at these meetings. Every gangster that showed up was an uncle, loyal to Dad and thus an unspoken protector of his wife and two daughters.

Before their discussions began, we were always told to go away and find Mom. I eavesdropped at the door, though, and this is how I started to almost fully comprehend Vietnamese.

Dad would map out the upcoming operation; stacks of cash were then counted and divvied up among the meeting's attendees.

When their business was complete, the guys would stick around to have a beer, coffee, or tea. The uncles played peeka-boo with Amanda and brought us lollipops and hard candies wrapped in plastic strawberry print. It was like they were real uncles. More than once, an uncle would slip a small bill into my hand and tell me to buy myself a toy. Some uncles were goofy, some were reserved, and some gave us teddy-bear hugs. When I look back, it's hard to believe that all of them were criminals.

The longer Dad eluded capture, the more pressure there was on law enforcement to find him. Dad became more paranoid; in any given situation, he was suspicious of someone or some-thing. "That car's been behind us too long," he would say as he turned off our course or slowed down to study the license plate of the car behind us. "You can always tell if it's a pig by the type of headlights on it," Dad said once, as if he was teaching me how to solve a math problem.

It was the most schooling I had gotten since we left with Dad. Although I was eager to experience the predictability of a full school year in kindergarten, I didn't want to trade chaos with my parents for stability without them. Whenever we reached our destination, we'd switch cars in a parking garage or several blocks from another parked vehicle in Chinatown.

When we went out to eat, he was constantly hyperaware of the customer traffic within the restaurant and the people outside of it. Dad would point out where he wanted us seated, and the waitstaff would quickly arrange tables, chairs, and dining sets to accommodate him. Dad always positioned himself so that the entrance, glass windows, and the majority of the restaurant were in plain view. His eyes would dodge from table to table, searching for an out-of-place face. A middle-aged White male sitting alone and fumbling through a Vietnamese-only menu would be the type of outlier that cut our lunch short, with a hefty tip tucked under the teapot before the waitress had a chance to bring us the check.

Cell phones were demolished as quickly as Dad put out cigarette butts, and all telephone calls had to be limited to sixty seconds or less. Dad preferred thirty seconds and would hang up on you by forty-five. He said that you ran the risk of getting tapped if you didn't keep it short.

During one phone call with his men, he stopped midsentence, pressed the cell phone to his ear, and then snapped the antenna off and started crushing it into the cement. Fractured plastic and loose wires embedded into the cracks of the pavement like roadkill. "Idiots!" Dad said through his teeth. "You don't keep talking when you hear clicking in the background!" He shook his head.

Rhythmic clicking was a sign that another line was attempting to tap into your call; it could easily be confused with a poor connection, especially since cell phones were still a newer technology at that time. The difference was that a poor connection cut the other person out; clicking from a tap didn't do that. The clicking occurred simultaneously to the talking, and you could hear both. Dad also said that if you listened carefully, the resonance of the phone call after the clicking changed, too, as if the person on the other end were suddenly in an empty building with high ceilings. It was all just another homework lesson to be learned.

10

For the better part of 1990, Mom, Amanda, and I kept up with Dad's pace as best we could, but being on the run with a six-year-old and a toddler hindered his efficiency. He had to delegate an uncle to drop off diapers and milk for Amanda. Her car seat had to be moved from one car to another, and she had to be carried since she couldn't reliably walk yet. Although having a sweet baby in one arm while holding his older child's hand was ideal for avoiding surveillance and shaping his image, the burdens of having us along were starting to outweigh the benefits. Mom and Dad agreed that on our next pass through the United States, we would stay in Massachusetts again while Dad secured his reputation as a bulletproof crime boss.

"I'll be back as much as I can," Dad said as he dropped our bags off inside one of his apartments outside of Boston. "Be good girls for Mommy." I nodded in compliance as I walked into the two-bedroom apartment on the third floor. The space was small. The entrance led straight into the dining room, which merged into the living room where there was a balcony over-looking the parking lot. I had my own bedroom, and Amanda shared the second bedroom with Mom.

He passed Mom a clean stack of bills held together with a rubber band. The cash ran out in a matter of weeks, and we were back in the same circumstances we'd been in when we lived in the townhouse: broke and helpless.

One rainy night, I was lying in my bed with the lights off, having a staring contest with the ceiling fan. I couldn't sleep, but if Mom said it was bedtime, I got into my pajamas, washed up, and went to bed whether I was tired or not. I listened as Mom put the dishes away in the kitchen, grabbed something from her room, and went to the living room. The TV switched on and the volume immediately lowered. She flipped through several channels before stopping at a Chinese soap opera. I pictured her on the couch, sewing an article of clothing and pausing now and then to read the subtitles. She had started learning Cantonese when she became fed up with Dad's family deceitfully switching between Vietnamese and Cantonese in her presence when they first started dating.

I was about to give in to slumber, hypnotized by the rotating fan blades and the dramatic soundtrack, when the clang of keys in the door snapped me out of my doze.

It was Dad, and I was excited. I had missed him so much. I had started collecting the leftover fabric when Mom hemmed his pants and kept it under my pillow to remind myself that he would be home to see me soon. I wanted to run out to greet him, but I was supposed to be sleeping. Maybe he would come in to see me. If he didn't, I could always pretend that I needed to use the potty and make sure he saw me then. Before I could play out my strategy, though, I heard shouting.

"Don't. Touch. Me," Mom emphasized by isolating each word.

"What's wrong, baby? Don't be like that. I missed you." I could picture Dad reaching for her as if nothing was wrong.

I hadn't heard his voice in a while. *I missed you too, Daddy*, I thought.

"Where the hell have you been?" Mom asked.

"I've been working. You know that."

"It's been over two weeks since you've been home."

"It took that long to get the work done."

"Oh, yeah? Bullshit."

"I told you. I've been taking care of things."

"But you can't even check in? You don't call. You haven't answered your phone or pager. Don't you care how we're doing? How your daughters are doing?" I thought about Amanda sleeping in the next room on Mom's bed.

"Of course I do. You know I have to take care of business so I can take care of us."

"Take care of us, how? You're never home. You haven't been paying the bills. We're on food stamps. Is that what you call taking care of us? Where's the money going, Trung?"

"I'm here now, Lon. That's all that matters."

"I asked you, where is the money going? To your friends? You gambling it away? Is that more important than keeping the lights on and feeding your family, you piece of shit?" I imagined Mom's lips shaking as she screamed.

"You'll get your money." Dad's consoling tone changed to indifference, which was usually a warning that he was losing his patience.

"Is it going to that bitch of yours, Sara? Is that where you've been?"

"It's over with Sara. How many times do I have to tell you that, huh?"

"You're a fucking liar. I'm not stupid!" Mom was getting louder. She must not have been sitting on the couch anymore.

"What do you want from me, Lon? I told you I was working. The money's coming."

"You're spending all your money on that slut! I know it. You're never going to take care of us. You don't give a shit about us!"

"Would I be here if I didn't give a shit?!"

Mom was quiet for a long moment and then said, "If you leave for that long again, don't come home."

I sat up in bed. He had to come home—come home for me!

"What did you say?" Dad demanded.

"I said, *Don't. Come. Home.*"

I wished she wouldn't say that. My nostrils stung like they always did before tears formed.

"I'll come home whenever I want to come home. Who the fuck do you think you are, woman? This is my place! Those are my kids! If I say it took two weeks, that's how long it took to get the job done. And if it takes longer, what are you going to do about it?"

"We'll leave you, that's what! We don't deserve this."

"Ha! You're not going anywhere." I could hear the arrogance in his voice.

Dad stormed down the hallway past my open bedroom door. The bathroom door shut, and the shower turned on.

Mom was still yelling as she chased him down the hallway.

"We don't deserve this, you fucking asshole!" She banged on the bathroom door after each sentence. "I hate you! I fucking hate you! You don't give a shit about us!" Screaming transformed into wailing until she was incomprehensible through her disheartened sobs. She walked away as he finished up in the shower.

When he was done in the bathroom, he came into my room and sat down on my bed.

"You awake?" he whispered.

I smiled as if I hadn't heard any of it and circled my arms around his chest. He was dressed. Fresh gel in his hair and the smell of his cologne relieved the stinging in my nares. "How're you doing, baby?" he asked.

"Good."

"I missed you so much. I miss you a lot when I'm gone, you know?"

I looked at him without any sign of affirmation.

"Do you? Then say yes. Say yes and that you know."

"Yes, I know." I hugged him again.

"I love you. You're my girl." He tilted my chin up. "Don't ever forget that."

"Love you, too."

"Daddy has to go back to work. But don't worry. I'll see you soon." He brushed the hair out of my face and kissed my forehead. "Go back to sleep now, okay?"

I curled up onto my side so I could see as much of him as I could.

Before he left my room, he started looking around and rummaging through my drawers and under the furniture. Then, his pager went off, and he snuck out.

"Why are you dressed? Where are you going?" Mom asked.

"Work. I'm not dealing with your bullshit tonight. And then you wonder why the fuck I don't come home." He went to the phone and dialed, presumably calling whomever had paged him. "Hello? Yeah, yeah. I'm on my way," Dad told them and promptly hung up.

"You can't leave us again. You just got back," Mom said.

"Where did you put that money in Ting-Ting's room?" he asked.

"Is that why you went in there?"

"I went in to see my baby. Now tell me where it is."

"No! That's all we have left. How are we supposed to survive? You can't take that. You have your own money. Isn't that what you said—that the money's coming?"

"I don't have time for this. I'll bring back all of it and more," Dad said as his pager beeped again. He returned to my bedroom and made another attempt to find whatever he was looking for in the dark. After a few minutes, he spotted a flimsy locked filing cabinet in the corner near the closet. It took three hard jerks before it busted open. Dad got what he wanted and slipped out again.

"You're not leaving us again, Trung! I mean it!" Mom shouted.

Then, there were sounds of a frenzy coming from the kitchen. I threw my blanket off and went to the edge of the doorway, where I could see most of the kitchen. Dad was frozen in place, looking up toward the cabinets. Mom stood on the counter with a knife at her neck. I covered my mouth, afraid I would make a noise.

"Whoa, whoa, Lon. What are you doing?"

"You can't leave! We have nothing! You leave us here to rot while you go party and spend everything on those whores! What about us?" she cried. "What about us?"

"Please come down from there."

"I will fucking kill myself if you leave. I can't do this anymore!" I had never heard Mom talk like this before. Dad hurt her all the time, but she had never once threatened to hurt herself. The thought of her slitting her own throat scared me more than Dad's abuse did. To me, that meant she no longer had the strength to fight or the endurance to survive. And if Mom gave up, there would be no promises left in this world for me and Amanda. I wanted the fighting to stop.

Dad's pager beeped again. This time, he silenced it without even looking at the number.

"Lon, calm down," he said. "It's okay. Put the knife down and come here."

"Is that what you want? You want me to kill myself?" Mom pointed the butcher knife toward the door. "Then leave. Go!"

I was trembling.

"No, I don't. I would never want that. Please, please, calm down," Dad said with his arms in the air, coaxing her to descend.

"Then don't leave! Don't leave us again, Trung," Mom begged. She sounded broken.

"Okay, okay. Let me call the guys back. I'm not going anywhere." Dad helped her climb off the counter, slid the knife out of her hand, and tossed it in the garbage. He held Mom close, rubbing her back and telling her that he loved her with each stroke until her hyperventilation subsided.

I exhaled when I realized that I wasn't breathing.

"You know I have to work, Lon." Dad swept the hair out of her face. "Look at me. I won't be long this trip. I promise."

She shoved him away in shock. "Fuck you," Mom said like a snake spitting venom. She hurried to the closet and put on her coat.

"Where are you going? What do you think you're doing?"

"What does it look like I'm doing? I'm leaving. You stay here and take care of your kids." With that, she walked out the door.

He started to go after her but hesitated. "Shit," Dad mumbled. His pager was going off at shorter intervals now. He grabbed the phone and dialed a number. "I'm on my way," he muttered, hung up, and rushed past me to the bathroom.

I tiptoed to the living room, where the television was glowing and a pair of Dad's dress pants lay disheveled on the couch. I looked out to the parking spaces we used from the balcony doors, scanning for our car—and for Mom. I spotted the sedan, confirming to myself that she wouldn't leave us.

A knock on the door reassured me. It was Mom. I was sure of it. I opened it to see a dirty blonde in a pencil skirt and peacoat standing there with a tissue and swollen green eyes.

"Hi." She wiped her nose and fixed her posture. "Um, is your dad here?"

Before I could answer, Dad appeared.

"Sara? What are you doing here?"

"Can we please talk, Peter?"

"You can't show up here like this."

"I know, but I really needed to talk to you."

My gaze darted between them.

"Go downstairs. I'll be down in a minute," he said.

"I know you have a family, Peter, but I love you. Can't we work it out?" Her freckled cheeks became flushed. "Did I do something wrong?"

"Okay, shh, shh. It's okay. Just go downstairs and we'll talk," Dad said, shushing her. She put her head down and walked away.

He went to the phone and made another call. "Hello? Look, I can't leave right now. There's no one here for my daughters. I'll be there as soon as I can."

I stood there, watching in confusion. My feet felt heavy, like they had welded into the floor.

"Okay, baby," Dad said to me. "Listen, you stay here with your sister, okay?" Amanda was not even two years old. The fiasco of the night had not disrupted her. "I'm going to go get Mommy. I'm not going very far, just outside. She'll be right back. Stay here. Don't go anywhere. She's gonna be back in a minute."

When I peeked in on Amanda, she was on Mom's bed, sleeping on her stomach. Her knees were snug underneath her body, propping up her tush. I sat down, careful not to wake her as the mattress puckered, and waited for Mom.

At some point, Amanda and I must've been carried to the apartment two units down and across from ours. We woke to the smell of sandalwood and the face of an old Chinese lady. She had soft eyes and straight silver hair neatly pulled back with bobby pins. We had run into her a few times with Mom since we'd moved in. She was a widow, and I never saw her without her round jade earrings and matching floral pajamas. Living alone with little to do, she had offered to keep an eye on us, and every once in a while, Mom dropped us off at her apartment. Now, after Mom and Dad had stormed out the night before, we would be spending the next week with her.

I learned later that after the blowup, when Mom walked out of the apartment, she decided to go home to Vietnam. She already had her passport, since she and Dad had been regularly traveling to Canada, so she borrowed money from a friend and booked the next flight to Saigon. She had to find her family, visit a Buddhist temple, and rid herself of the toxic energy that was accumulating in her life.

After she arrived in America, Mom had had access to postal mail and had written letters to her mother and siblings to reassure them that she was indeed alive. After running away with Dad, those letters ceased. The letters her family sent her were returned to Vietnam, and after a while, they stopped writing too. It had been over five years since Mom had lost touch with her family.

INTERLUDE

As the third of seven children, Lon was a mischievous girl with the heart of an eternal optimist. Her family lived in Saigon, which later became Ho Chi Minh City when North Vietnam won the war and changed the metropolitan's name in honor of the prime minister. Lon's father ran a rice and soy sauce factory, in addition to working some odd jobs outside of his business, as her mother stayed home to look after Lon and her siblings.

At the time, the Vietnam War was all around her in one form or another, causing decay in South Vietnam with violence and fear. Yet part of her found the chaos exhilarating: the whistling of a bomb along its trajectory, the explosion as it met the ground, the hysteria of hundreds of screaming people rippling out from a rising cloud of smoke. In the early 1970s, at as young as six or seven years old, Lon felt like she was on the set of an action movie, skipping school to observe fair-skinned men dressed in fatigues and strapped with weapons. Going down to the waterfront was the highlight of her misconduct. She would sit and watch, her legs hanging from the pier, as colossal steel ships drifted weightlessly on emerald water. If she was lucky, a sailor or two would give her a high five or greet her in English. "Hello," Lon would respond in a sweet accent. The sight of a handsome face under the brim of a navy hat always made her blush.

On occasion, when she slipped away from her desk and out of the classroom, she would run into her father while en route to her next adventure. "Hi, Ba!" she'd exclaim cheerfully.

He would lift her up, twirl her into a hug, and give her a nuzzle on the cheek.

"Aren't you supposed to be in school, young lady?"

She'd shrug as he placed her back on her feet. He'd then ruffle her hair into a mess, kiss the top of her head, and remind her to be home for dinner.

Lon's father wasn't the type to reprimand her or any of her siblings. Skipping a few days of grade school was nothing in light of the grandiose plans he had for his family. He was going to give them the gift of opportunity. Locked away in a safe was a backpack he had prepared for each one of them. Inside was one bar of gold, nonperishable army food, and an extra set of clothes. Her father had made all the necessary arrangements for them to immigrate to the United States. The backpacks were in case they got separated, whether in the war zone or while on the way to America.

But not long before their planned departure, Lon's father died while working on a US Navy ship. There was some suspicion that his death was no accident and a result of his entrepreneurial efforts. In private, some even called it an assassination, as he was killed instantly by a single fatal gun-shot to the neck. The suffering was saved for his family.

Even after her father's death three years earlier, eleven-year-old Lon continued to play hooky and go to the waterfront. One particular evening, much to her delight, a small ship was docked below the pier. It wasn't one of those enormous steel vessels. It was more like a wooden dinghy, but it still intrigued her, none-theless. She glanced in both directions and discovered a ramp at the rear end of the boat. *I wonder what's inside.*

Before letting the thrill of the moment ignite her to action, she paused to see who was around. She froze as a group of Americans passed her on the boardwalk, uninterested in their attention. As soon as the sound of their foreign tongues was washed out by the noise of the city and the shore, she skipped onto the ramp and ran into the ship.

It was murky and damp inside the boat. The smell of stag-nant salt water and moist cargo made her feel sticky. Still, with unbounded curiosity, she wandered throughout the ship's hold, hoping to make her way up to the deck. Then, a beam from the setting sun above outlined the silhouette of a staircase. She ran over, climbed halfway up, and squatted down when she spot-ted men on the deck. Lon had thought the boat was vacant. When she heard more people, she ran back down the stairs and hid behind them. The voices grew louder and multiplied. The activity up on deck became busier until it was apparent that she wouldn't make it up to the deck today without being seen. *Maybe tomorrow.* She started heading back to the entrance she had snuck in through. Then, the rumble of the motor shook the hold, throwing her off balance. She picked up her pace toward the exit. Before she could get near it, a herd of people began to board through it, and she dashed behind some cargo to hide. As more figures entered the hold, she realized that their whispers were in Vietnamese. She was now enclosed by Vietnamese women and children.

The confusion didn't slow Lon down. She pushed against the crowd, squeezing between bodies and boxes with her eyes fixed on the way out. Before she could reach it, though, the opening disappeared. Her body stiffened as she sensed the undulation of moving water. The commotion of passengers succumbed to the roaring waves as the shoreline faded into the horizon. A tragic mishap resulted in Lon suddenly leaving her family behind and voyaging to another country alone.

11

Dad came to see us every other day during our stay with the Chinese lady. He came over unannounced, knocking on the door but barging in before she could open it and get a good look at who it was.

"Are they doing okay?" he asked the woman as he picked up Amanda and rubbed my back.

"Yes, fine," she said, closing the door.

He put Amanda back on the floor and sat on the edge of the couch.

"So, their mom should be back soon, okay? I can't take them with me," he said, bouncing his bent leg up and down, like a nervous twitch.

She didn't ask any questions and told Dad that she could watch us for as long as they needed.

Dad smiled uneasily and got up. "It shouldn't be much longer. Maybe a few more days. Page me if you need anything," he said as he jotted down a number. Then he showed himself out before I could get a word in, leaving as hastily as he had arrived. I turned to my sister with the same grin that Dad had given the woman. I sat close to Amanda and showed her how to line up the dominos on the floor. With more attention than usual, I played with her, hoping to make up for our parents' absence, or, at least, to distract her from it. Looking back as an adult, I handled the situation with patience that was out of proportion to my age. Like a cub in hibernation, the mayhem was kept inside of me in a dark and deep place, allowing me to conserve energy in order to survive the coming adverse conditions. I internalized the confusion and reflected composure. I took each morning as it arrived, losing trust in my parents as daylight vanished. I secretly prepared to be Amanda's keeper.

One afternoon, Mom came to get us. She'd been gone for about a week and looked drained. I resisted the joy I felt when I saw her, careful not to tire her out even more. Her eyes seemed withdrawn and defeated, as if she had traveled halfway across the globe for insight and came back empty-handed. She thanked the old Chinese lady and walked us back to our apartment. We hung out in the living room until dinner. Amanda cruised along the furniture in nothing but her diaper.

Mom lit incense and arranged oranges, grapes, and Asian pears in a bowl on the mantle before our Buddhist statues. She arranged three sticks of sandalwood incense upright in a cup of rice in front of Buddha. Then she placed another stick by itself in front of Guan Yin, which I had never seen her do before. Gowned in white, sitting cross-legged atop a lotus pedestal, with a willow branch in one hand and a vase of pure water in the other, Guan Yin is the deity of mercy and compassion. The name "Guan Yin" translates to "she who observes all sounds of suffering in the world."

It didn't matter how many times we moved or how short our stay was, from what I remember, Mom always kept a symbol of Buddhism and incense in our home. The tribulations she faced were relentless: separation, immigration, abuse, poverty, abandonment, heartache, and betrayal, like the edge of a cliff collapsing underneath her grip one finger after another. As her fingertips calloused and her nail beds lifted, Mom's faith in karma offered her a flicker of reassurance. The downward fall wouldn't destroy her, and good fortune was coming.

Once the incense was lit and arranged, Mom closed her eyes, clasped her palms together, and said a silent prayer. The ash crumbled and fell between the grains of rice as a pirouette of smoke floated upward. I discreetly put my palms together, bowed my head, and said my own prayer: *Please, please, give Mom whatever she may be praying for.*

Whereas all of Dad's family had immigrated from Vietnam by the 1980s, Mom's family never followed after her unexpected departure. The plans made for their evacuation disintegrated with her father's death. They never heard from the man who was supposed to smuggle them out of the country together. Rather than follow Mom, they were left to endure the tragic aftermath of the Vietnam War. After a while, when she failed to come home, they finally assumed that she was dead, until a letter arrived on their doorsteps signed by Mom.

When Mom had arrived at the Malaysian refugee camp on Bidong Island, she had had no other choice but to live in a makeshift hut composed of salvaged timber and trash, rationing food and water with strangers in unsanitary conditions. She had searched for her sisters and brothers in the crowd as each boat unloaded another group of Vietnamese refugees.

Eight months after arriving in Malaysia, Mom was informed that she had been sponsored by a group of Americans in the suburbs of Boston. She lost all hope of reuniting with her family as she journeyed across the Pacific Ocean. By the time she arrived in the United States, her skin had contracted over her bones, her joints ached, and her once-voluminous hair was brittle from severe malnutrition. Six months later, she met Agnes Schafer.

INTERLUDE

Lon had been in the car for hours. She still could not believe that she had held a knife against her neck and threatened her own life just last night. This was wildly uncharacteristic of her. That was when she knew something had to change. She hypothesized and analyzed every scenario to get her family away from Peter safely as the driver went from one place to another. When she realized that her childhood address no longer existed, she offered the driver US dollars to help her find her family. They drove through the streets of Ho Chi Minh City all the way out to the edges, asking anyone around regarding where her family may have wound up. When someone mentioned that the family moved west, where many city inhabitants did after the war, they started driving toward the countryside. As they approached the Cambodian border, there was a small town on the Hau River called Chau Doc, where they narrowed down their search. Lon knocked on doors, greeted by unfamiliar faces, and asked strangers if they knew of a family with a widowed mother and five children. Lon's youngest brother had died from malnutrition during the war when her mother couldn't find baby formula anywhere. Without him and Lon, only three sisters and two brothers were left.

It was very common to live where you worked in Vietnam. You had your business in the front on the ground floor, ate in the back room, and slept upstairs. Lon approached a rice warehouse and recognized her older sister. They locked eyes. "It's me. Loan Anh." Her sister stiffened and turned pale as if Lon had risen from her grave and called to her other sisters and brothers. The sight of Lon sent everyone into shock. Behind her siblings, her mother sat in a chair, stoic and detached. "You're not my daughter. My Loan is dead."

After the war, many children became orphans and homeless. They would pretend to be a missing family member to seek shelter, and this is what Lon's mother believed was happening. The excitement fell silent, and everyone was motionless. Lon walked up to her mother and rolled up her shirt sleeve, exposing her entire right arm. Rough patches of discoloration littered up her forearm and coalesced into a large area over her deltoid and shoulder. This was Lon's unmistakable birthmark. Her mother's eyes traced the feature and reached her face. Tears flooded, and Lon sank into her open embrace.

12

Mom's trip must have stunned Dad.

"You can't just leave the country like that," he said, biting the bottom corner of his lip, as if worried she would do it again. "I can't take care of the girls and do what I do. They need you here." Under any other situation, Dad would have been furious at Mom's exodus, but this was the rare instance that he was able to express empathy, as short-lived as it was.

"It's hard for me to take care of them, too," Mom said. "Especially without any money, help, or family. Even if I got a job, who would watch them? Felicia needs to start school soon. She can't miss out on any more."

Dad scratched his temple as if he understood the dilemma.

"We'll go to Canada for now and figure things out," he suggested.

With no other reasonable solution, Mom packed our stuff, and we headed for the border. The skyline of Toronto was brilliant as we drove. Metropolitan lights sparkled as they reflected off Lake Ontario and fused to create abstract art on the surface of the water. The CN Tower was like a pin on the city and reminded me of a structure that King Kong might scale. On the outskirts of Chinatown, we arrived at our new condo, a luxury space with a view filled with skyscrapers.

For two or three days, we hardly did anything. We watched TV, Mom cooked, and Amanda and I entertained ourselves with what we could find, which was a deck of cards and an abacus. Dad made minimal phone calls and didn't even leave the house. I started to think we were finally settling down.

It was well past midnight when thunderous pounding on the door woke us all up. Amanda cried out as Mom ran into our bedroom and hushed us both. I was disoriented, not knowing if I should stay still or start getting my stuff. Mom gripped my arm and told me to be quiet. She didn't seem flustered at all, and her focus grounded me. I could hear myself breathing as she rocked Amanda back and forth, soothing her.

"RCMP! Open up," a booming voice demanded, identifying them as Royal Canadian Mounted Police, the federal and national police force of Canada.

The pounding continued, and I held on to Mom as Dad scrambled to hide rolls of cash and a gun. There was no other way out of our place.

"RCMP! We know you're in there, Truong. Open the door."

The pounding on the door grew louder and gained momentum until the hinge buckled and the door whipped open. Half a dozen men in uniform busted into the condo. Two of them seized Dad; one cuffed his wrists while his partner, dressed in a suit and tie, recited Dad's rights. The other men began flipping mattresses and cushions and ransacking cabinets and drawers as they raided the place. I looked at Dad on his knees and thought that this would be the last time we saw him. I'd had this thought before, but there was something about this moment that felt different as I centered my gaze onto his face. For a split second, I felt relief. Unlike in the past, Dad wasn't leaving us, and we weren't leaving him. He was being taken away, and having no choice eliminated the emotions. I wasn't scared. I wasn't sad. It felt tolerable.

Mom carried us both across the hallway into another room before we were seen. I saw a tremor in her hands as she shuffled through a pile of papers on a desk. She stopped when she came across three blue passports. She grabbed them and cowered with us in the far corner.

An officer entered the room and called over to the others. "A woman and two children in the building," he said looking us over. "Are you guys legal?"

Mom said that we were as she relinquished our passports. He inspected them with his flashlight and handed them back over.

They escorted Dad out and left the condo in single file, kicking the mess out of their way as they went. Amanda was still crying. Mom was still shaking. We sat among the wreckage, holding on to each other so tightly, it was like we had merged into one being. I wondered if it would ever be safe to let go.

An uncle picked us up at dawn and drove us back to Boston.

As it turned out, there had been a shooting at a nightclub in Toronto earlier that night, caused by a silly conflict that had blazed out of control. The men involved were Dad's men, linking him to the crime scene, which was enough to authorize a warrant for his arrest. Uncle reassured us that he would get to the bottom of this and keep us posted.

He carried our bags into the townhouse—it was the first time we had returned here since we had left it to go on the road—and asked if we needed anything before he left us. Before Mom could decline, she hit the light switch. Nothing happened. We all looked up at the bulbs. She flipped the switches nearby. There was no sign of luminescence. Unfortunately, it wasn't uncommon for Dad to miss paying the utility bills if he was out of town for a while.

"I'll try to get this taken care of before I leave town," Uncle said as he walked around and tried the rest of the lights. "It's not a lot, but it's all I have for now," he said, removing a few bills from his wallet and giving them to Mom.

I recalled the day we first moved into this townhouse. The thrill of seeing Mom again after they had left me with my grandparents for almost a year, of meeting my baby sister, and of spending the night in our new home as a family had been a dream come true. Just as other kids my age wished for bicycles and trampolines, I yearned for a dad eager to tuck his girls in at bedtime and a mom who would stop hurting. How fleeting that feeling of happiness had been. The bright white walls now seemed to be stained gray, the open loft ceiling seemed hollow, and the dandelions in our backyard seemed lonely, waiting to wilt into a tuft of feathery bristles and be blown away to freedom.

We all slept in the same bed that evening. Mom was wedged in the middle with me and Amanda on each side. I was exhausted but couldn't sleep. Instead, I gazed at Mom faintly snoring and Amanda fast asleep with her little legs sprawled across Mom's torso. I was puzzled by how serene they looked, given the events of the last twenty-four hours. The threat of separation haunted me; the sound of pounding on the door echoed in my ears; Dad's unbothered facial expression was clear in my mind. I covered my head with the blanket to block out the noise and sealed myself from the darkness.

Go to sleep, I told myself. *You will forget about it by tomorrow.*

13

Morning came, and I spent a few minutes trapped in a bed of tangled sheets and lopsided pillows, stretching before joining Mom and Amanda in the common area. Natural light poured into the living space, filling it with creases and shadowy corners. Mom had removed all the curtains from the windows and the sliding glass patio door, and for a moment, I forgot that we didn't have electricity. Oddly enthusiastic, she was cleaning out the refrigerator by throwing away rotten food and scrubbing the surfaces. Her hair was tied back, and she wore yellow latex dishwasher gloves.

"How'd you sleep?" she asked when she noticed me.

"Good." I sat down on the cool kitchen tile with Amanda, closing the cabinets behind her as she opened one after another.

"I have to go out today. I need to see what's going on with the lights and pick up some food," she said, unfazed as Amanda pushed on the refrigerator door, trying to close it with Mom inside.

"Can I stay here while you do that?" I didn't feel like going anywhere. I was drowsy, still dazed from the previous day's turmoil, and the thought of even the slightest stimulation gave me anxiety. My forehead was tense, and my body felt heavy. I needed a break, an uninterrupted moment to lose myself. A few hours of mindless cartoons or a coloring book would have been the ideal antidote.

Mom tilted her head, as if she were about to question me. Perhaps she would bring up what had happened, ask me how I was coping, or provide an uncomplicated explanation for all the chaos. Instead, she just said, "Sure, I'll take your sister with me." She tied the bag of spoiled goods and trash and took it outside.

Mom was gone for the rest of the morning and most of the afternoon. I didn't consider the fact that without electricity, there was nothing to do. There was no television, no radio, and nothing to eat. There was one book in the house, but I had read it cover to cover twice, including the fine print on the publication page. When we previously lived at the townhouse, Mom would shoplift books for me, even more advanced ones since I could already finish a thirty- or forty-page book in one sitting. Then she discovered that library cards were free. Not returning properly checked-out books was much easier than hiding them in the waist of her pants and holding her breath as we exited the store. I probably had almost a dozen books, but between dropping one in a hurry, Amanda tearing the pages out of another, and forgetting them in a car or apartment that we never went back to, only one remained here.

I twiddled my thumbs and began to regret my decision to stay home. Then, I started thinking about Dad and what he did for "work." I had thought about his line of work before, but I never had the nerve to ask questions. I knew he had business in multiple cities, needed a bunch of phones, either had a lot of money or none, ran meetings with men who were supposed to be my uncles but not real uncles like Uncle Vincent, and was constantly on call via a pager. I had simply accepted our lifestyle, like most other children would. However, witnessing the raid and, specifically, Dad's nonchalant face and Mom's poise during the ambush really made me want to know more. We had visited him in jail before, and I had just watched him get arrested and taken away. This wasn't normal. If police officers went after bad people, lying was reprimandable, and hurting your family was wrong, then there must have been an explanation.

My conclusion: Dad was a bad guy who was doing bad things. He called those bad things "work." I wondered if a bad person could still be a good parent, a good dad, if his bad actions weren't intended for me. Then I thought about how Dad made me feel, and my shoulders slumped. My chin lowered and I noticed the sound of my breathing inside of my chest. Dad mostly made me feel sadness, disappointment, and doubt. Any joy he offered me felt shallow and temporary, as impermanent as a Popsicle on a scorching summer day. I would only get a small taste before it all melted away and left me with a mess.

Query after query about my dad arose in my mind, and before my imagination could construe a logical answer to one of them, my curiosity would set another avalanche of questions in motion. Unknowns inflated my head like a balloon stretched thin and on the verge of explosion. I exhaled to let the air out.

I jumped up with a sudden sense of urgency. If I wanted answers, it was time for me to start snooping around.

The grown-ups didn't disclose much of anything to me, and it was a sign of disobedience to ask them too many questions. Plus, Dad was not an easy guy to talk to. When I did ask him questions, he often pacified me with vague comments.

"There's a lot of bad guys out there after your daddy, okay? Guys that want to see your daddy go down. But that's not going to happen, baby. You know who your daddy is?" he would say with a cocky grin.

I decided to search the house for whatever the officers in Canada might have been looking for, and the only room worth searching was my parents' bedroom. Aside from my items in the loft upstairs, the remainder of the townhouse was vacant, with just a couch, TV, and dining table in the open space.

The shades were still drawn in their bedroom from the night before, so I pulled the beaded chain to expose about a third of the window, letting in enough light for me to see what I was doing. Starting with the bureau, I opened each drawer from top to bottom and sifted through unfolded clothes. To hide any trace of me digging through their belongings, I tried to leave the mess the way I found it, with garments hanging out so the drawers couldn't be shut. Next, I went over to the dresser that was taller than me. I pulled over a folding chair from near the closet so I could inspect the dresser thoroughly. On top, there was a sewing kit, some pens, several scrunched-up receipts, and a torn piece of paper with Vietnamese written on both sides. More unfolded clothes, socks, and underwear were in the top two drawers. The others were no different. Hidden under the dresser was a dog-eared picture of Dad holding me on a clear summer day, taken a couple of years earlier in Boston's Chinatown. I swept my finger along the photo, removing a thin layer of dust. Right there, in that moment, we appeared normal, like a regular dad with his regular daughter, out and about, enjoying a regular day. We seemed to have a bond that wasn't real outside of that perfect picture. I stared at us for a few more seconds and then slipped the photo beneath the dresser.

Under the bed was an empty, black, zippered duffel bag, some scattered change, and a ripped envelope with a Malden, Massachusetts, return address. I was starting to get discouraged. I glanced at the closet with its sliding mirrored doors. It was probably just more disorganized clothes, but I was going to finish what I'd started.

Dress shirts, pants, and Mom's blouses hung lifelessly from the hangers. An ironing board stood upright at the far end. At my feet were shoes, an extra set of bedsheets, belts, and pocketbooks. I displaced the heap and found a white, square cardboard box with cutout handles on the sides. I raised the lid; it was filled to the brim with a thick stack of papers. Jackpot. I pushed the box over to the window. I sat down and got comfortable with my back facing the window so the light would shine onto the pages. Finally, something to read.

The first pages were basically blank. I flipped through the papers one at a time, turning them over and placing them facedown on the floor to make sure they remained in the same sequence. I skimmed through several more pages that contained Mom's name, various dates and locations, random letters and numbers arranged like code, and words like "indictment," "defendant," "jury," and "court." There were also words like "conspiracy," "armed robbery," and "assault and battery." There were eventually long paragraphs as well, but the legal jargon was far too sophisticated for me. I continued to flip through the documents, licking my thumb when I lost sufficient friction, like I had seen Yeh-Yeh do when he read the Chinese newspaper.

Then, a change in font and texture of ink caught my eye, and I started reading.

"I'm sorry, Ms. Thai. Please speak up so the courtroom can hear you."

"Can you repeat the question?"

Unlike a book, where a narrator guides you through the dialogue, noting who said what, this was more like a script.

"Were you or your husband, Truong, at the scene of the armed robbery that took place at Phnom Peng Jewelry Store in Lowell, Massachusetts, on October 17th, 1986?"

"No, sir."

"Do you recall where you were on that day? Please speak up, Ms. Thai."

"Yes. I was at the doctor. My daughter had an appointment that day."

"Was your husband with you?"

"He drove me to the appointment. Yes."

I frowned in confusion, skipped the trivial scribe notes, and read more. This back-and-forth exchange echoed conversations I had overheard during Dad's various meetings.

Mom was on trial here. She wasn't testifying for Dad. I felt sure of it, but I couldn't be certain. Were police after them both?

There was no way I would get through all these papers before Mom got home. I grunted. I had to do something. But before I could sneak a handful of pages upstairs to the loft, I heard Mom unlocking the front door. I replaced the papers and straightened them and then jammed the lid on the box and put it back where I found it.

A couple of days later, the box was gone.

14

The Commonwealth of Massachusetts versus Loan Thai.

My mom had indeed been on trial in that transcript. In fact, she was convicted on charges of conspiracy to commit armed robbery, as well as assault and battery by means of a dangerous weapon. They were the same indictments that Dad had faced and been convicted of. The jewelry store owner had identified Mom as the female robber on that infamous day and even accused her of picking up a hand mirror and striking the store owner's wife across the face with it.

One month later, an anonymous message provided the court with the name of the true female robber. New expert evidence also became available, demonstrating that the fingerprints on the mirror did not match Mom's. In light of this information, the Commonwealth of Massachusetts filed a *nolle prosequi* and dropped all charges against Mom. I was one year old at the time and destined to avoid every attempt the universe made to take her away from me. It was a twist of serendipity that had started with the day Mom walked out of that abortion clinic.

Dad also got lucky. Mom and Dad had told the same story when questioned on the stand: that there was no way either of them could be at the scene of the robbery, since they were taking me to a wellness checkup. At the time of the trial, there had been no corroborating evidence that I had a doctor's appointment, and his alibi claiming that he had picked us up from Malden to drop us off at the pediatrician's office in Boston didn't check out. But then, Dad's lawyer obtained medical records documenting my doctor's visit on October 17, 1986, at two o'clock, which stated that I was present and accompanied by my mother at the scheduled hour. An evidentiary hearing to introduce the discovered information was granted and the appellate decision on Dad's case was reversed.

A year following this dismissal, Dad was arrested again. He was charged with and found guilty of another armed robbery in Lowell. This was the crime for which Dad only served thirteen days behind bars before breaking out of prison, which ultimately led us all to Canada the first time.

Now, with Dad's arrest after the RCMP's raid in Toronto, we thought it was the end of the line for him. A week later, we were proven wrong. The RCMP didn't have anything on him. Aside from a lengthy interrogation, which was interrupted by his lawyer, Dad came out unscathed. In Canada, he was a free man, and the United States was out of their jurisdiction. He was coming home.

15

When Dad got back from being detained by the RCMP, things were different. Mom could hardly look at him.

I started attending elementary school in the middle of first grade. Mom looked for work, and Dad went back to his mob business. Dad's older sister, Aunt Lana, was a manager at a Chinese restaurant not too far from our townhouse, and she offered to hire Mom until she found something more stable. Mom didn't take on many shifts before getting a job at the Gillette factory in Boston doing low-wage assembly line work. Finding childcare wasn't easy, though, and at seven years old, I was taking care of myself and babysitting Amanda when I was home from school. She was three, and Mom's shifts were long.

Mom did her best. She was earning an income, keeping the lights on and our tummies full. We were still collecting food stamps and sporadically had to shoplift small things that we needed. We depended on Dad less and less, separating our identities from being his trophy wife and kingpin family. It was natural for me

to follow Mom's lead when it came to Dad. If she was upset with
him, so was I. If they weren't speaking, I kept my distance from
him. And if they were okay, I showed him guarded affection. As
I got older, my attitude toward Dad became independent from
the perception of their volatile relationship. I missed Dad, but I
was learning I couldn't trust him, so rather than fluctuate on the
spectrum between love and hate, I became apathetic. I started to
detach my emotions from him the way birds abandon their nests
when it appears as though their habitat has been disturbed.

We started spending more time with Aunt Lana as Mom's
relationship with her grew. Aunt Lana was married and had two
sons and a daughter, all in their teens. At the restaurant, she
made sure to comp our meals, and she even expressed a bit of
empathy for what Mom was going through with Dad. "He was
always the crazy one, Lon, but inside, he's a good man. He loves
you and the kids. I'll talk to him."

Our visits to her house increased, and when finding childcare became difficult, Aunt Lana said I was welcome to stay
there. Her kids were old enough to look after me, but Amanda
needed more supervision, so Mom dropped her off at the house
of a friend who stayed at home. "They're cousins," Aunt Lana
said of us. "Family. Ting-Ting can come anytime."

I didn't know them well enough to consider them family.
I only had brief interactions with them at one of Dad's fam-
ily functions or simultaneous visits to see my grandparents.
Mom thanked her, though, and I soon became acquainted with
Kenneth, Vivian, and Tony.

"I shouldn't be long," Mom said to me as she dropped me
off at Aunt Lana's house one day. I clung to her leg; my hands

wrapped around her thigh. "I'll be back later tonight—tomorrow at the latest." When I didn't budge, she prompted, "Say hi to Aunt Lana, Felicia."

"Don't worry. Take as much time as you need. I have a shift at the restaurant tonight, but the kids will be home," Aunt Lana said.

"Okay. Thanks a lot."

"And tell Trung to call his sister every once in a while. Geez, I'm always worrying about him! He better be staying out of trouble," Aunt Lana said, rolling her eyes as she escorted Mom out to the driveway.

When Aunt Lana returned, my feet were still in the same spot.

"I'm going to be working at the restaurant tonight. Okay, honey? Kenneth is in the back, so he and the other two will watch you while I'm gone. Why don't you go find them?" With that, she guided me farther into the house.

Kenneth was her eldest son at eighteen years old. Vivian was two years younger than him, and Tony was a year younger than her. I walked away, pretending to look for Kenneth, but softened my steps as I got closer to his room, hoping he wouldn't know I was here. Aunt Lana went back to her bedroom to get ready for work, and I slid into the den and onto the couch. I stared at the distorted reflection of myself on the television screen, wondering how long it would be before my cousins noticed that I was in their house.

Aunt Lana came out of her bedroom with dark eyeliner, her pale complexion splotched with rouge.

"You couldn't find them, huh?" she asked while putting on her earrings. "Kenneth! Vivian! Tony! I'm going to the

restaurant! There's leftovers in the fridge. Ting-Ting's here, too."
I cringed at her announcement. "See you later!"

When I heard the door close and lock behind Aunt Lana
and the car ignition start, I wanted to run and hide, but there
was nowhere to go.

"When did you get here?" Kenneth asked, sauntering
into the den. He was a lanky guy with long buck teeth and a
spotty mustache.

"A little bit ago." I scooted back into the corner of the couch.

"Hey, guys, come out here," Kenneth yelled to his siblings.
He plopped down next to me, turned the television on, and
started changing the channels.

"Hey, Felicia," Vivian said, entering the room.

Tony followed behind her, and we all squeezed onto the
couch. We watched as Kenneth flipped through the channels so
quickly we couldn't see what was on before he clicked away again.

"There's nothing good on." Kenneth turned the TV off and
slammed the remote control down on the coffee table. "What
should we do?" He looked at me and then over at the other two.
His underbite gave him the look of a villain.

"Whatever you want. Eric and Emily are coming over later,"
Vivian said. Those were my other cousins, and I felt a light relief
knowing they would be here soon. They were the children of Dad's
younger sister, but I rarely saw that aunt. Their family was different and somewhat sophisticated compared to the rest of us. After
immigrating with Dad's family to the United States, she entered
college, earned her bachelor's degree, and married an educated
Chinese man. They both had stable jobs with steady income and
were able to save for a house in a safe middle-class neighborhood.

At a rational time, they started a family of their own and were blessed with a son and daughter. She was the quintessential example of the American dream, and she kept her interactions with Dad at a minimum to protect her accomplishments.

"Hmm, okay. How about . . ." Kenneth got up, pulled my legs up, and twisted my body until I was facedown. "We pile up on Felicia!" He jumped on my back, and the other two piled on top of him. They jerked up and down, forcing the air out of my lungs and making it impossible to inhale.

"I can't breathe," I squealed between impacts.

The laughing grew louder.

"Please. Really. I can't!" My vision got blurry under the weight of three grown bodies. "Please!" I gagged and let out what felt like my last breath, and they got off.

"Stop being such a fucking baby, Felicia. We're just having some fun," Kenneth said.

The three of them walked out. I lay there hyperventilating. I wanted to cry, but I knew that if Kenneth heard a peep, he'd come back for more. I'd learned that early.

When I was at Aunt Lana's house, I had no one to protect me. For a few days each week, I had to protect myself until Mom returned. Sometimes, I prayed that my uncle would save me. I wished that I knew him, but he was more like my aunt's husband than an uncle, and I was never sure if he was home. I had seen him emerge from his dim bedroom once or twice. Dressed in an oversized wifebeater and slippers, he dragged his legs to the kitchen to grab a beverage. Then, he meandered back into the bedroom like a raccoon, passing me without acknowledgment.

If I told an adult and my cousins got in trouble, they

would know I snitched. If they found out, I was convinced they would try to kill me.

The thought of bringing it up to Mom didn't cross my mind. I figured she wouldn't be able to do anything about somebody else's children, so why stress her out and add to the burdens she carried? Therefore, I decided to handle my own distress and tried to tell Aunt Lana about her kids' abusive behavior toward me. I had carefully considered my options for help, and she was a reasonable and, perhaps, sole option for me. Aunt Lana was scheduled to work a late shift, so she was there most of the day. I trailed behind her like a stray pup while she cooked and cleaned.

"Don't you want to go play with your cousins?" Aunt Lana asked, noting me standing by the counter as she rinsed the dishes.

"Umm, not really. I can help you, if you want," I said, leaning toward the sink.

"It's okay, honey. But this is boring. Why don't you go find them? You guys can play video games or hang out. Whatever you want."

"I don't want to." I looked down at the open dishwasher.

"So, you want to stand here while I load the dishes?"

"Yeah. Sometimes . . . I don't like playing with them," I said, keeping my eyes low.

"Why not?"

"Mmm . . . because."

She turned off the faucet, closed the dishwasher, and looked at me as she dried her hands, waiting for me to continue.

"Because, uh, because they hit me sometimes, Auntie."

"My kids what?"

I hesitated and then decided to take the risk.

"Not Vivian and Tony. But Kenneth does. I'm scared to play with them."

"They hit you?"

"Uh-huh."

"My kids hit you," she said, as if to confirm what I was saying.

"Just Kenneth, really."

"Mm-hmm. So, is it all of them or just Kenneth that hits you?"

"Usually Kenneth. Unless he makes them do it, too."

"Are you sure?"

"Yeah. I don't want to play with them, Auntie."

We stood face-to-face now.

"They would never do that to you, Ting-Ting," she said. "My kids would never hurt you."

My face fell, and I looked down at the floor.

"It's not nice to lie about your cousins. If you don't want to play with them, fine, but making up stories so you don't have to?" she said. "I'm disappointed in you."

"I'm not lying," I mumbled.

"It's not nice," she repeated. "They watch you and babysit you when there's no one around to take care of you. Not even your own mother. You wouldn't want me to tell your mom and dad that you're lying, would you?"

"No."

"All right, good. Now go find them. I'm going to lie down before my shift tonight." With that, Aunt Lana hung up the dish towel and left the kitchen.

Now what? My fear magnified. All that for nothing. If they found out, I was a dead girl. But maybe that was better than what I was now. Right now, I was a helpless girl susceptible to physical pain and tortured by pure dread. I felt lost, as if I had been dropped deep in a forest with a blindfold on. When I untied the blindfold, assuming it would help, it was the middle of the night, and every path I took was as hopeless as the next. All directions led to nowhere, and when I looked up for guidance from the stars, the tops of redwood trees obscured the constellations. I wanted to lie down on the ground, rest my limbs on the soil, close my eyes, and disappear.

16

On a late afternoon after being dropped off at Aunt Lana's house, I quietly entered the dwelling and stayed in the mudroom for a long time. I almost dozed off on a pile of shoes when the creak of the door startled me. I sat up, hoping to see Mom, but it was my other two cousins, Eric and Emily.

"Hi, Felicia." Emily gave me a big hug. She was a sweet, pudgy, five-year-old girl with flat, silken hair.

"Hey," Eric said. His arms were rigid, and his hands were buried in the pockets of his jeans. Eric and I were both seven, just a few months apart. He liked to spike his hair straight up with gel and had light brown puppy-dog eyes.

The six of us joined in the common area.

"What're we doing tonight, guys?" Kenneth asked as if he already knew the answer to his own question. No one replied, but I could tell that Vivian and Tony were in on whatever scheme Kenneth had come up with. It was written all over their faces.

"Well, we made up a game for Felicia and Eric since they're both seven now. It's gonna help toughen you guys up," Kenneth said.

"I wanna play." Emily leaped up with her hand in the air, as if eager to be selected by the captain of a dodgeball team.

"No, Em. You're too young to play. Go to the back playroom and play with the toys there," Kenneth said.

"I wanna hang out with you guys, though," she whined.

"What did I just say?" Kenneth said, clenching his jaw. "You're playing back there tonight."

Emily pouted, but she knew better than to talk back, so she moseyed down to the playroom. I was jealous of her. I wanted to be too young to play these games. I would've traded my soul for that two-year difference.

"Let's move to the other room so we have more space." Kenneth opened his arms and waved us in the direction of the shrine room. The only things in there were a red oriental rug and a counter against the wall where bowls of ripe fruit and burnt incense sat in front of Buddhist statues.

"Felicia, you go stand over there." Kenneth pointed to one side of the room. "Eric, go to the opposite side." We stood in our corners as if we were inside a boxing ring. Vivian and Tony sat against the wall across from Buddha, and Kenneth was in the middle of the room, explaining how the game worked. "The game is easy, and the rules are simple. You two are going to fight each other. You're gonna fight in rounds. We'll decide when you need a break and determine who's the winner," Kenneth said like some kind of referee.

"Come on, Kenneth. Why?" Eric asked. "Why do we gotta do this?" He had the courage to question Kenneth's insanity. I admired his bravery, but knew he wouldn't change Kenneth's mind, only piss him off.

"Because both of you are fucking pussies, that's why! You need to learn how to fight or else you're gonna get your asses beat up in school or on the streets. So just shut the fuck up and do it," Kenneth barked.

"You're fighting a girl, anyways, Eric. So why are you complaining?" Vivian chimed in.

"All right, let's go." Kenneth clapped his hands together and sat down between Vivian and Tony, scooting forward to get a good view.

We didn't move from our corners as our older cousins perched on the carpet like spectators.

"Let's fucking go!" Kenneth repeated.

"Yeah, I'm not trying to be here all night. Do what he says and get it over with," Tony said, shaking his head like this was a waste of his time.

Tony was a quiet kid with a careless attitude. He wasn't scared of Kenneth, especially as he got closer to his brother's size, since most of their confrontations were violent. But even if Kenneth beat him black and blue and left him limping, Tony would walk away like he didn't give a shit. He picked his own fights and left ours alone.

Eric and I met each other in the center of the floor.

"What are you guys waiting for? Hit him, Felicia," Kenneth urged. "Do it."

"Hit me," Eric whispered.

I pushed him. He shoved me back, and I punched him in the chest.

"You're letting a girl beat your ass, Eric. You fucking pussy," Kenneth said. His siblings cackled.

Eric punched me back. I braced for the impact and the onset of pain and then realized that his fist didn't land very hard. After that, we started to act out this so-called game with heavy throws disguising light-handed blows for their entertainment.

"Hit him harder, Felicia! Like you mean it," Kenneth snapped. He got up and pushed us apart, his demeanor suddenly changing. He got close and hovered over me. He was double my height. He lifted his shirt and looked down at me. I broke eye contact for a brief moment and noticed the Buddhist figures in my peripheral vision, as if they were watching us, too. "Hit me like you mean it," he said.

I struck him in the stomach and winced as soon as my knuckles felt skin.

"Harder! You're gonna have to do better than that! Harder!"

I let loose and hit him again. And again. I kept swinging until I was hot in the face and could feel sweat on the small of my back.

"That's what I'm talking about!" Kenneth hollered like an amped-up football player. "Hit Eric like that!"

As I panted and let my arms dangle like skeletons' limbs, he made Eric do the same thing.

"Now that you know what I want, you're gonna start over." Kenneth returned to the audience.

Eric was scorching red, and his eyes glistened with anger. He looked like he was both going to cry and charge into the wall at the same time. "It's okay. Just do what Kenneth says. I'll be okay," he said.

We both knew that this game wasn't going to end unless one of us played by Kenneth's rules, and Eric had deemed me the player. I cringed as I began hitting Eric as hard and as fast as I could. But he wasn't hitting me back; he just shoved me away. Hysterical, I rebounded and continued assaulting Eric as if I were striking Kenneth instead.

Kenneth cheered in amusement.

Eric gave me one last vigorous push, and I fell to the floor. For a second, I thought I heard myself weeping. Then, I looked up to see Emily at the room's entrance, sobbing into her hands.

"I told you to stay in the back playroom!" Kenneth scolded. "I told you, you're too young for this game."

Emily ran away. It was late in the evening, too late for Mom to come pick me up tonight. But the game was finally over, and we were still alive.

17

If there were adults present, I had to be around them. It was a survival strategy. I'd tell them that I was hungry so they would fix me something to eat, and then, I'd chew my meal slowly. I'd show interest in what they were doing, hoping they would offer to teach me solitaire or let me watch their favorite TV series with them. I'd insist on helping with the chores, like taking out the garbage or doing yard work or folding laundry. Any task that kept me occupied in the same vicinity as an adult was the safest scenario.

If there were no adults around, I gravitated to Tony or Vivian. Tony mostly avoided Kenneth, and Vivian did what she could to stay on his good side. If Kenneth wanted to torture me, I couldn't let it be alone. Tony and Vivian did not protect me. In fact, under the influence of Kenneth and to avoid being abused themselves, they bullied me, too. Both of them seemed like they were afraid of him, but unlike me, their fear was limited. They were Kenneth's true family. If the sky came crashing down, the three of them would have each other's backs. The difference was that the evil within Kenneth didn't exist in them. I held on to the belief that, with enough pity and empathy, they would intervene in truly awful circumstances. So, if Vivian or Tony had to leave the house for any reason, I wanted to tag along.

"You want to come with me?" Tony asked, surprised.

"Yeah. Please. I wanna come. Whatever you're doing, I'll be good," I said.

"All right." He smirked. "But you can't say shit to anyone about it."

I sat in his car and watched him demolish another car's windshield with a baseball bat and break off the rearview mirrors. A few days later, when Aunt Lana asked me about it, I told her that we had gone to the grocery store to pick up some Cap'n Crunch.

"I want to come, Vivian," I said another night.

"I'm meeting up with my man and his friends, so no," she said as she braided her hair, watching her reflection in the mirror.

"Let me come. It sounds fun. I'll be good."

"You're not coming looking like that."

I ran off and changed my clothes.

"You can't say shit to my mom," she warned when I returned. "My boyfriend is Puerto Rican."

I sat at the dining table in someone else's house, surrounded by high school students drinking and smoking while my cousin made out with her guy for hours. She talked about him the whole way home.

A few days later, when Aunt Lana asked me about it, I told

her that we had gone to Vivian's girlfriend's house so she could copy notes from history class since she had been out sick.

I attempted to gain their trust like this and forge a genuine relationship with them. My intuition kept telling me that Kenneth would take it too far one day. It was only a matter of time. And when that time came, I prayed that they would be my saving grace. Except they weren't.

18

"He's on 'E,'" Vivian said in a matter-of-fact tone one evening when she, Tony, and I were sitting around in one of the bedrooms.

There were three beds in that room, a set of bunk beds and a twin. Vivian and Tony were on the top bunk with their heads hanging over the edge. I could see them from the bottom bunk as I listened to their conversations. Kenneth wasn't home.

The last few times I'd been dropped off, Kenneth had left shortly after his mom went to work and came back acting weird. He would be staring into space and smiling for no apparent reason. The oddest part was that he teased and pushed me like normal, but as soon as I thought his anger would turn vicious, he relaxed and burst into laughter. He wasn't as aggressive as he usually was, and eventually, he'd retreat to his own bedroom for the night. It was disturbing and a relief at the same time.

"What's that?" I asked, confused by Vivian's comment.

"Ecstasy. It's a drug," Tony said, glancing down at me.

"It makes you wanna have sex," Vivian said, covering her mouth to smother her laugh.

"You're stupid," Tony said, grinning himself.

"It does! That's what he told me," Vivian said. "Don't tell him we told you, Felicia."

"It makes you wanna have sex?" I didn't get it.

"Yeah, like horny," Vivian tried to explain.

I still didn't understand.

"You don't need to know." Tony rolled his eyes.

Vivian was still giggling to herself. I wanted to join her, but I held it in and continued listening to them chat. Vivian did most of the talking, rambling on and on about her boy-crazy high school drama while Tony insisted that the guys she liked were all losers. When Kenneth wasn't around, they were my cousins; when he showed up, they became my predators.

"He's so lame, Vivian, with his bright-ass Reebok jumpsuit," Tony said of one guy she brought up.

"No, he's not! He's cool! You don't even know him," Vivian yelled. "He's sooo cute!" She rolled onto her back and dangled her hair over the side of the bed so that it swung in front of me. I wondered if we would ever brush each other's hair or if maybe she would teach me how to braid.

The sound of Kenneth entering the house silenced all the foolish chatter. The bedroom door busted open, and he walked in with that peculiar expression. "What's up? What the fuck you guys doing?" He hopped onto the lower bunk bed next to me.

I slid over to the foot of the bed, keeping my back pressed to the wall.

"Not too much." Vivian straightened up.

"What about you? What you been up to?" Tony asked.

"Nothing. Popped some 'E,' though," Kenneth said as he lay down at my feet and looked up to the upper bunk. "Feeling good right now."

"Oh, yeah?" Tony said, unimpressed.

"Yeah." Kenneth turned to me. "You know what 'E' is?"

"No." Vivian and Tony were tuned in to my answer.

"Stand over there and I'll tell you what it is." Kenneth thrust me off the bed.

I got to my feet. Vivian and Tony were looking down at me from above and Kenneth stared at me, his eyes bloodshot and eyeballs twitching from side to side.

"It's a drug," he said.

I wasn't sure how to react and grew uneasy as the three of them watched me as if I were a circus animal expected to perform a trick.

"I told Vivian what it is. Right, Vivian?" Kenneth broke his stare to peek up at her. "Tell Felicia what it is."

"It's a drug . . . a pill that makes you want to have sex," she said, this time with less conviction.

Kenneth erupted in laughter.

I looked up at his siblings. They looked at each other, both seemingly as confused as I was. We all waited until he calmed down.

"Take off your pants, Felicia," Kenneth said.

"No!" I tugged my pajama pants up high on my waist, not understanding what he wanted with them. He leaned in toward me, and I took a step back.

Kenneth dropped his head in frustration.

"Take them off for a minute, and you can put them right back on," he said.

I shook my head no. When he lifted his head, I shook it frantically to make sure he saw me.

Unfazed, Kenneth came forward and yanked my pants down.

"Stop!" Like a knee-jerk reflex, I dropped to the floor and pulled my pajamas up so high, they wrinkled in my crotch and you could see my calves.

"What are you doing, Kenneth?" Tony asked.

"Shut up," Kenneth said.

Tony jumped off the top bunk and left the bedroom.

Kenneth started laughing again. "All right, I won't do that again. I was just playing. You can get back on the bed." He sat back and patted the mattress beside him.

I didn't move.

"Come on, I told you, I was playing around. It's okay. Get back on the bed."

I still couldn't move.

"Get back on the fucking bed, Felicia. I'm not gonna do it again." His neck strained as he insisted through his teeth.

"Kenneth, chill," Vivian said. "You heard him, Felicia. He won't do it again."

My heart was pounding in my ears. I approached the bed but wouldn't get on. Kenneth slapped the mattress once. I climbed onto the lower bunk. The metal frame and upper bunk seemed to cage me in. The springs creaked above, but Vivian was out of sight.

"Why are you so scared? I'm not gonna do anything to you."

Kenneth lifted his legs onto the bed. "Just take your pants off. That's all." Folding his arms behind his head, he let out a melodramatic yawn. Maybe this drug was wearing off. He started to recline onto the pillow.

Suddenly, Kenneth launched himself at my ankles and forced my legs straight. One hand ripped my pants off while the other pulled the back of my underwear. I turned onto my stomach, my bottom exposed and my underwear twisted as I tried to keep my genitals covered. The last piece of fabric slipped from my grasp. I clenched my eyes tight and stretched my T-shirt down, but I couldn't cover up. I buried my face in the comforter and heard Vivian climb down from the top bunk. The door shut behind her. *Not you, too.* Boiling tears seared down my cheeks.

Curtains dragged across my mind, closing out the world and leaving the details of what happened next hidden in black shadows within my memory.

It was dark when I woke up in the single twin bed, drenched in an onerous energy. The bunk beds were empty. The house was silent. Beneath my blanket, I was naked from the waist down. There were no clothes to be found in my bed or anywhere nearby. I ran to the dresser to put something on. Then, I curled up underneath the sheets and meticulously swaddled them around me so not an inch of my skin was exposed.

In the coming years, the seams of toddler underwear were tattooed along my bikini line as I outgrew them. We couldn't afford new undergarments, so I squeezed into the two-sizes-too-small panties. I didn't mind, though. It didn't matter how much they bunched up or if they dented my skin from being too tight.

They were my layer of protection. Even the thought of not having them on made me feel violated.

On days when I was brave enough, I tried to pull what had happened to me from the shadows. My heart rate would pick up, the fine hairs on my forearms would slant upward, and my brain would start to feel numb, as if all the blood had drained from my head. Yet I could carve out no clear images or trauma. There was only an intense compulsion to contract every muscle fiber in an attempt to protect my body.

Was it considered betrayal if they never had your back to begin with? If there was no intention of supporting me and no interest in defending me? My expectations of Vivian and Tony were unrealistic, but I was forced to hold on to them anyway. Alone, in that house with those people, there was nothing else. As Kenneth became more of a monster, I combatted the horror and coped with my fear by transforming Vivian and Tony into my guardians. They laid off me after that night. Kenneth conveniently wasn't home during the days I was there or had last-minute plans as soon as I arrived. Vivian and Tony avoided me too. I didn't know how to explain what happened to myself, so it didn't make sense to try to explain it to anyone else. Not even Mom. So I gathered every recollection of Kenneth's attack from my mind, took them down to the basement of my subconscious, and hid them away.

19

By 1993, between Boston, Montreal, and Toronto, Dad was bringing in over a million dollars a year in illegal revenue. He had also added heroin trafficking to his resume. We had no idea where the money was going, since we saw none of it. I rotated through the same three outfits each week, and we opted to walk places rather than drive to save on gas. Nothing got easier. Mom and Dad still fought whenever he came home.

"I don't want this life anymore!" Mom screamed at Dad as I walked through the door after school one day. "I don't want to be with you anymore!"

"You want to be with someone else? Is that it, huh? Is that why you need new clothes and to put on makeup?" Dad demanded. He got louder and closer with each question.

"You're sick in the head, Trung." Mom dug her index finger into her temple. "I'm out here doing the best I can, 'cause you don't do shit for us! And that's never going to change."

"What do you want? You want money? I'll go get you money right now, you greedy little whore!" Dad struck the wall.

"Ha! Greedy? Look at us. Look at your kids!"

I was still standing by the door with my backpack on. Amanda was curled into the corner of the couch, clutching a pillow to her chest. Dad didn't look at us.

"You're the greedy one!" Mom spat. "I'm tired of your stupid lies." Mom shook her head in defeat.

Finally, Dad noticed us, as if we had just appeared out of thin air. "Hey, baby," he said to me. "How was school? Come over here."

I looked at Mom and didn't move.

"You mad at Daddy now, too?"

I didn't say anything.

He called over to Amanda, "Come here, baby. Give Daddy a hug."

Amanda crept over and warily put her arms around his neck.

"See? Your sister's not mad at Daddy. But it's okay. You can be mad," he said with a smug expression. "You really love your mommy, huh?" He let go of Amanda and turned back to Mom. "Okay, listen. Let me go into the city. I'll come back and give you what you need."

Mom ignored him.

After Dad left, Mom suggested that we go over to her friend's house and "get some fresh air."

We drove fifteen minutes to a house with vinyl maroon siding and white shutters on a rounded corner that gave way to a cul-de-sac. A soft-spoken and warm Asian woman slightly older than Mom welcomed us. Steam whistled from a teakettle. The woman introduced herself as Ming. She filled two porcelain teacups and sat down at the island counter with Mom. Mom told us to go play outside while they chatted.

With little money for toys, Amanda and I had developed quite the imagination. When we were home alone while Mom was working, one of our favorite games was "the jungle." We'd take the cushions off the sofa, place chairs in random places around the living room, and leap from one piece of furniture to another as if they were cliffs or lush trees. If we didn't land on padding, we could fall millions of feet into the unknown. We collected rainwater in the palms of our hands and sought shelter under enormous elephant ear leaves. We clung to each other while balancing on a dining chair as blazing hot lava from a volcanic explosion flowed toward us. We took turns being rescued from the inferno as our footing slipped on the wet precipice. In the wild, we had no voices and had to communicate with our eyes and gestures in a language that no one else understood. I lit shreds of newspaper on fire in a cooking pot so we could keep warm at night. It was a game of survival, and we always came out together. And alive.

Today, we frolicked on the front lawn of Ming's house, turning cartwheels and sniffing her hibiscus blossoms.

"Let's climb that tree!" Amanda said, pointing. I followed her gaze to a broad trunk with low-hanging branches, typical of the New England landscape, but I saw a tropical rain forest reflecting off her irises. We ran over to the tree and began to climb. The bark shed under Amanda's little hands. "I can't get up," she said.

I leaped off the branch and boosted her up into the tree. We sat gleefully on a swinging limb.

"I'm a monkey!" Amanda dropped upside down with her arms and legs wrapped around the bough.

I giggled and moved into the same position. Mom came outside.

"Look, Mom! We're monkeys," Amanda said. Our hair hung down like a troll doll's.

"Oh, my goodness! How did you guys get up there?" Mom laughed as she rocked the branch, swaying us. She helped us down and announced that we were staying for dinner.

As we were setting the table with plates and utensils, Ming asked Mom if she was expecting someone. Mom was not. Confused, they peered out through the window. I climbed on the couch to look as well and saw Dad in the driveway. My body tensed.

"I have no idea how he knows we're here," Mom said. "Don't answer the door, Ming. I don't want you to get involved."

The doorbell rang, followed by forceful knocking. I got off the couch, hugged Amanda, and looked at Mom for instruction.

"Why don't you take the girls to my room," Ming said.

"I know Lon's here. Open the door," Dad shouted, hammering the door with his fist.

Ming waved us off as she approached the entrance. She secured the door's chain lock before opening it.

"May I help you?" Ming asked.

"Who the fuck are you?"

"A friend."

"Get Lon out here."

"She doesn't want to see you right now."

Dad rammed into the door, straining the chain. Ming slammed it shut and latched the bolt. Dad went berserk, pounding so hard it felt like the roof was vibrating. "Lon, get out here! Get out here!" he screamed. "Get out here with my kids!"

Ming huddled with us. She kept her face impassive, but I could tell she was trying to hide how frightened she was. Her eyes darted, and she jumped each time Dad hit the door.

Glass shattered, and we heard the door unlock from the inside. Ming looked ashen.

"Where the fuck are you, Lon?" Dad's footsteps were inside the home now. He wandered in and out of rooms. "Get out here!"

A thunderous crash startled us, and Mom ran out of the room. I tugged at her pant leg and tried to stop her. Dad was in the meditation room, violently sweeping his arms across the mantle and demolishing the Buddhist statues. More than a dozen gods and goddesses shattered on the floor into unrecognizable forms, including Buddha himself.

Dad caught sight of Mom. "Where's Ting-Ting and Yeem Kwon?"

"What are you doing?" Mom yelled, scanning the broken fragments.

Dad bulldozed past her and discovered me and Amanda crouching beside a bed, almost under it.

"Come on. Let's go. You're coming with Daddy," he barked.

We were paralyzed.

"Get up, Ting-Ting. Come on. Grab your sister. Yeem Kwon, it's time to go."

In sloth-like motion, I rose to my feet. I was Amanda's protector, but in this moment it felt like I was leading her to harm, to the lava. Against my will, I signaled to Amanda, gesturing that I would keep her safe in our own language and led her toward Dad.

"Where do you think you're going?" Mom was behind him.

Dad grabbed the front of her shirt and yanked her face up to his. "Don't you ever fucking try to take my girls away from me again." He threw Mom against the wall, and she fell to the floor in the hallway.

We got into the back seat of Dad's car and sped off. Amanda was distraught, sobbing uncontrollably for Mom. I stayed quiet until the turbulence of the car ride started to alleviate—a sure sign that he was calming.

"Where are we going, Dad?" I asked in a low tone looking at him via the rearview mirror.

"Home, baby."

"What about Mom?"

"She'll be back."

"I want Mommy!" Amanda cried.

"I'm your dad. Why are you scared to be with your own daddy? There's nothing to cry about. I would never do anything to hurt you. We're just going home."

I was surprised when Dad actually took us home. It was strange to be with him without Mom around. He told us to go relax as he went to the stove and started boiling rice. Thirty or so minutes later, he beckoned us to come eat dinner, which consisted of rice porridge with dried pork sung, chopped green onions, and soy sauce.

"Daddy can cook, too," he said. "You didn't know that, did you?" He raised his eyebrows at us.

I stirred the contents together, taking small bites. "Go ahead, baby. Eat."

"We want Mom," I said.

"What do you want Mom for? Daddy knows how to take care of you guys."

Amanda started crying again and refused to touch her food. I passed her a napkin and told her it was okay. "She's going to come home," I said, stirring her porridge and blowing on it so it wasn't too hot to eat. "Don't worry."

When Mom came home that evening, Amanda and I hugged her as if she had been torn away from us permanently. By now, Dad was showered, shaved, and dressed. He was restless and paced the living room like a windup toy. He looked at his watch and then at Mom, and the quarrel continued.

Mom called him psychotic, and Dad accused her of trying to steal his children from him.

"When did you start caring about being around for them?" Mom scowled when he didn't respond. Dad stepped out for a smoke.

Mom tucked us into our twin beds and told us to get some sleep, despite looking like she needed rest more than we did. Her makeup was smudged at the rims of her eyes. Her lips were chapped. The collar of her shirt was loose and sloppy, wrinkled by Dad's grip. "There's nothing to worry about," she reassured us before kissing us good night.

Amanda and I lay on our sides facing each other, awake and alert. We could overhear everything downstairs from our loft. Dad was outside on his phone for a while, his conversation stifled. When the sliding door opened again, Mom said, "We need to talk."

"What is it?"

There was no answer. I heard Mom sniffling.

"What do you want to talk about?" Dad asked again.

A deep breath in. "I'm pregnant."

There was no noise.

Then, a pressured sigh from Dad. I could picture his nostrils flaring. Then, the sliding motion of a chair relieved from the weight of a body. Then, the door latch, opening and then shutting without a hint of hesitation.

I looked at Amanda. She was asleep, her mouth slightly ajar and her cheek cupped in her palm.

It was silent for a while after Dad left. Eventually, I heard Mom retreat to her room. Intermittent sobs snuck out through the doorjamb and floated into the loft. I squeezed my eyes shut and focused my attention on that room, as if I could move objects with my mind. I wanted to transfer Mom's pain to me and take on her tears. If I could bear her agony just this once, then I would prove to myself that I was suitably tough to carry it all.

When I was in second grade, my elementary school had a raffle for various gifts in honor of Mother's Day. Raffle tickets were handed out to all the students. At lunchtime, a teacher picked ticket numbers at random and announced the winning numbers over the PA system. There were three prizes: flowers, chocolates, and a pie.

When the teacher called out the winning numbers, I examined my ticket carefully and then raised it in the air. I had won the pie. I was overjoyed. I didn't know what flavor it was or what filling it had, and I couldn't care less. I kept the pie with me for the remainder of the school day and held it tightly as I carried it home. There was a pep in my stroll as I anticipated surprising Mom with the pie. I was so excited to give her something.

When I got home, I took off my shoes and put my backpack down. I placed the pie on the dining table with pride, as if I had baked it myself.

"Hey, Felicia. How was school?" Mom asked.

I waited for her to notice the pastry. I didn't have to wait long.

"What's that?" she asked.

"It's a pie. I got it for you for Mother's Day. I didn't want to wait until Sunday to give it to you, because I don't want it to go bad." I nudged the pie toward her. "Happy Mother's Day!"

Mom loved it. She loved it even more when I told her that I'd won the pie at the school raffle. She kept telling me how lucky I was, that she couldn't believe that out of all those raffle ticket numbers, mine had matched, how I must have a lot of fortune coming my way.

For as much as she loved that pie, we never got around to eating it. Mom didn't have much of a sweet tooth. It sat on the table well past Mother's Day until the custard dried out and the crust hardened. We treated the pie like a lucky charm, a pleasant reminder to not lose sight that something good could happen.

Giving Mom a gift brought me a sense of euphoria I had never experienced before. It was a brand-new interaction between us, a lovely feeling based on her reaction and my gratification. I had a hunch that the world had robbed Mom of what she deserved, thus owing her an enormous debt of happiness.

INTERLUDE

Lon walked up the steps of the temple. She had taken an impulsive trip to Vietnam after threatening to kill herself in front of her husband. A bead of sweat formed just below her nose, and strands of hair were pasted to the back of her neck as the humidity hung in the air like fog. Jet-lagged and sore from the flight, she had stopped at the temple immediately after leaving the airport. She slipped off her shoes as she approached the pagoda. Green shingles met at corners that curved skyward and were held up by clay red pillars. Intricate golden patterns shimmered as they caught the sun.

Hands clasped, Lon bowed at the sight of a passing monk and entered the place of worship. A soothing chant vibrated within stony walls, and sandalwood smoke spiraled toward the divine. She lit two sticks of incense, held them to her forehead, and repeated her prayer. *Hail to the jewel in the lotus.*

Lon prayed to be cleansed of all negative energy and aligned with harmony, to rid herself of suffering and welcome peace and healing. She also prayed for the strength and love of a son. She vowed that there would only be one father to all of her children, a deep-seated value established during her upbringing.

Lon bowed three times and set the incense before Buddha. She sat at the foot of the shrine and gave into meditation.

Lon touched her belly as a cramp radiated into her lower back. Her abdomen tightened and became hard like a watermelon's rind, taking her breath away. When the contraction subsided, she was able to fill her lungs again and reach for the telephone. Trung's cell phone went directly to voicemail. She dialed him again. Then once more.

"I'm having contractions. Call me back," Lon finally informed the voicemail.

She hung up and got herself a glass of water. She sipped the cool liquid and contemplated driving herself to the hospital. She looked around for her purse and keys, but her body stopped her at the onset of another contraction. She clutched the edge of the counter until her knuckles went pale.

As the pain tapered off, Lon shuffled through a drawer, pulled out the local phone book, and made her way back to the landline mounted on the wall. She flipped through the business section, navigated her way to the end of the alphabet, and guided her finger down the listings. When she found what she was looking for, she made another call. "Hello, I need a taxi please. I'm going to Goddard Memorial Hospital."

Hours later, on that warm August evening in 1994, she gave birth.

"Congratulations, it's a boy," the nurse said, placing a shrieking and swaddled bundle on Lon's chest.

Lon locked eyes with her son, and for an instant, the monitors silenced and the bland hospital walls transformed into red and gold oriental paneling carved with images of lotus flowers and Bodhi trees, recreating the tranquility of a temple. It was a flash of collateral beauty that gave her hope.

"Is there anyone you would like us to call?" the doctor asked.

"No, thank you," she said without disturbing her bond with Bryan.

20

By 1994, Dad had managed to avoid the authorities for nearly seven years since escaping the prison in Shirley, Massachusetts. But the murder of a rival gang leader that summer led to his ultimate downfall.

Phong Ly had become involved in racketeering in Boston and had encroached on Dad's territory, so Dad was obligated to show him which crime boss was in power. He and his gang planned the assassination for weeks. Dad obsessed over the details of the execution, found all the firearms, and plotted the exit strategy, which routed down Tyler Street in Chinatown.

On August 27, 1994, Dad and his gang were informed that Ly was expected to be at a local gambling den. They lay in wait outside. When his gang's weapons misfired, Ly became aware of his attackers and took off running through the streets. Dad became enraged and ordered two of his gang members to go after him. Two men fired a total of six shots at Ly as they chased him down and killed him in public.

Six weeks later, an FBI surveillance team patiently anticipated Dad's arrival outside of a restaurant in Revere. When he
drove up, he was instantly surrounded by flashing blue and red
lights. Dad stepped out of his car with his hands up in surren-
der. He was arrested for conspiracy to commit murder.

Dad was arraigned about a year later in October 1995
and ordered by the judge to be held without bail. Unlike his
prior charges for criminal acts under state law, this was a federal indictment—*United States v. Truong.* The trial was held at
the United States District Court, District of Massachusetts in
Boston. From there, it would take almost three years to wrap
up the trial proceedings before a grand jury and for the case
to be closed.

We pulled up to stained concrete walls. Looped barbed wire
stretched across the top of the barricade like an overused slinky.

We had been visiting Dad in jail for about a month after
the arraignment, but our visits were getting shorter, and the
intervals between them were getting longer. The last time, we'd
spent more time making the drive and getting through security
than being with Dad.

Mom turned in to a parking spot and stopped within the
painted lines. In delayed motion, she shifted the gear into park
as if a hijacker in the passenger seat held her at gunpoint and
she was trying to stay composed. As she turned off the ignition,

I unbuckled my seat belt, reached over for Bryan in his car seat, and poked Amanda to let her know we were here. I started to zip up the diaper bag, but Mom stopped me.

"You can leave that here, Felicia," she said. She got out of the car and slipped Bryan's car seat over her forearm. I held Amanda's hand as we entered the brick building.

"Which inmate are you visiting today?" a sturdy woman asked.

"Trung Chi Truong."

"All right, I'll need your ID. Please fill this out with the names of all the visitors with you." She passed Mom a pen and clipboard through a slit in the glass window between them. "Then, get in line for the security check."

Once Mom had filled out the form, we got in line. She placed her keys and purse on the belt that led into a large scanner. Shoes, jackets, and sweaters went next. Mom carried Bryan and the car seat through the metal detector and joined our belongings. We walked through one by one and then stepped to the side to be patted down. By this point, Amanda and Bryan were usually crying, but security wouldn't let us near one another until the screening was complete. Mom soothed us with words while strangers in uniform frisked her, her legs in a wide stance and her arms straight out. Bryan was stripped, his diaper was checked, and we were free to proceed. We gathered our stuff, exited the far side of the building, and entered the prison grounds. I ran across the field of stale grass to meet Dad.

"Hi, baby," he said, taking my hand. Together, we walked back toward Mom.

We all sat down on a cracked bench, with splinters jutting from the bone-dry wood. I studied the area, a large open space enclosed by wire fencing and opaque barriers. Two or three men in uniform guarded each portal, and everyone else was in dull tan jumpsuits, including Dad.

I examined him. A midline fold tugged at his eyebrows. His jumpsuit was much too loose and hung from his bony joints like fabric pinned on a clothesline. His olive skin was speckled with blemishes like craters on the moon. His teeth were tinted with the residue of Marlboro Reds. Yet despite all this, Dad was still handsome.

"When are you coming home?" I asked. "Do you live here now?"

"Daddy's coming home soon, okay? You don't have to worry about nothing. Daddy will take care of you guys and Mommy. It doesn't matter where I am. I'll always take care of you," he said.

"But don't you want to come home with us?"

"Of course I do, baby. I miss you guys. A lot of bad guys want to keep your daddy here, but I don't want you to worry. Your daddy is a tough guy, you know." He cracked a smile. "I'll be home soon."

Mom glared at him. I wished that the both of them would stop lying. I was ten years old, but Dad still spoke to me like I was a baby.

"Soon like when?" I asked.

"Soon, baby." He patted my shoulder.

"Soon like when, Dad?" I pressed.

"Daddy loves you. You know that? You know how much I love you?" he asked.

I looked away.

"Do you? Do you know your daddy loves you more than anything?" he asked again.

I couldn't tell if he was trying to convince me or himself.

"When are we going home, Mom?" I asked.

"Go play with your sister," she said.

We left a gap between them as I took Amanda over to the rickety merry-go-round.

It seemed misplaced, a miserable and desultory attempt at a playground on spotty dead grass and weeds. Amanda got on the platform while I pushed the bars to get it spinning. When I built up enough momentum, I jumped on, but the merry-go-round came to a screeching stop when my weight was added. After a few more underwhelming cycles, we both lounged on the motionless carousel.

"Push us, Daddy!" Amanda shouted as Mom and Dad approached. "Push us!" She was hopping up and down, jolting me with each landing.

"Careful, honey," Dad said. He gave us a couple of half-hearted spins and then told us to get off. "Mommy's tired. It's time to go home." He knelt down. "Come give Daddy a hug."

Amanda and I gave him a group hug, and he accompanied us to the building we'd come in from. When he wasn't allowed to go any farther, he tickled Bryan, told him to be a good boy, and chuckled.

Dad kissed Mom on the cheek as we departed and told her he would call soon. I wouldn't see Dad for another eighteen years.

21

Mom cut ties with Dad's family after our last visit to him behind bars. This included my grandparents, Uncle Vincent, and Aunt Lana. With Dad locked up and his followers being arrested one by one along the East Coast and up into Canada, his gangs dissolved.

Without the already small amount of assistance we had received from Dad, his family, and his gang members, Mom struggled to care for three young children. When the electricity was cut again, we couldn't get them to turn it back on. And when the eviction notice came, Mom moved us into a five-hundred-square-foot apartment in the projects, taking with us what furniture we could fit. Our apartment was on the third floor of a run-down red brick building at the top of a creaky stairwell. If you turned on the light in the kitchen at night, cockroaches scurried away into every nook and crevice. Whenever it rained, the living room ceiling became bogged down and blistered by a water leak, dripping onto our carpet.

On one of our final nights in the townhouse, we sat on the floor, trying to salvage the last few hours of sunlight before dusk. Mom fidgeted and scratched at her cuticles, as she did whenever she was stressed. Bryan tripped and got up again as he practiced his wobbly steps from one spot to the next, entertaining himself as I played with Amanda.

As the shadows lengthened, we were interrupted by something that sounded like brisk, trickling water flowing from above. We looked for where it was coming from. Halfway up the stairs to the loft, Bryan was leaning on the banister, naked from the waist down, and peeing in between the spindles, aiming straight for us. Mom exploded in laughter. Amanda and I thought it was gross, but Mom was beside herself. She clutched her sides and toppled over, tears gathering at the corner of her eyes as she laughed harder. Bryan was giggling from the stairs. Soon, Amanda and I started cracking up, too. We laughed until our abs were sore, and no noise could be heard coming from our mouths.

"That's the man of the house from now on," Mom said as she stood up to fetch Bryan. She tickled and nuzzled his plump cheeks until he couldn't stand it anymore.

Although we never visited Dad again, we kept in touch with him by telephone. If the landline rang in our apartment, it was almost without a doubt a collect call from him. He updated Mom on his latest meetings with his lawyer, asked how we were doing, and encouraged Mom to attend the trial. "Come to the trial as my wife, Lon. If you can bring the kids, even better. The jury has to see that I'm a family man. It'll help my case."

Mom showed up at court for parts of the trial, but as it dragged on, she stopped going. She couldn't do it anymore. Mom couldn't justify spending her time and effort to help him—a man she not only no longer loved but was also starting to resent. She wanted to focus on raising her children and keep us away from being used as his props in court. Eventually, we stopped answering the phone, too. It would ring incessantly. A snip of the operator's voice would be recorded on our voicemail, a click indicating that the call had disconnected, and then, the phone would start ringing again. When the noise started to drive us insane, Mom unplugged the cord from the wall until we needed to use it. In rare moments of weakness, Mom told me to answer, and I accepted the collect call. This was not because she wanted anything to do with him but because she wanted him to have a chance to talk with his children.

"Hey, Dad. Mom's not here," I said, whether she was or was not.

"Where is she? Do you know? What kind of mother leaves her three kids alone at home? Who is she with? If Mommy were with another man, you would tell Daddy, right? You tell her that if I find out she's with another man, I'll find him!"

I let him vent about Mom's whereabouts and eventually would end the call when he failed to acknowledge anything else, like me, Amanda, or Bryan. He didn't ask to speak to them, and he only spoke to me because I accepted the call and I listened. At first, I would give him an excuse as to why I had to hang up the phone in a hurry; then I stopped answering it altogether. Again, the phone rang for days, and I became the gatekeeper between Dad and my family. Numbness set in like a fresh concrete pour, and he couldn't hurt me anymore. He couldn't hurt us anymore.

One day, Mom unraveled the telephone cord and stretched it across the apartment as far as it would go. "Why are you calling if you can't help us?" she demanded without any greeting, having deigned to accept Dad's call. "We have nothing, Trung. Do you understand that? Nothing! What am I supposed to do? What the hell am I supposed to do? Tell me! All you care about is yourself. You've never given us a damn thing. Don't call here again. Do you hear me? Leave us alone!" Mom slammed the phone down onto the counter, wailing as she melted into the kitchen floor.

22

As Dad's trial continued into 1996, my situation at home and at school became increasingly arduous. Mom was working two jobs, so I took care of Amanda and Bryan, who were now six and almost two, after school and on the weekends. I was about to turn eleven years old. Dad was on the local news constantly, and journalists were following the trial in the newspapers. I was growing apprehensive at school, paranoid that my teachers knew who my dad was. It wouldn't have been difficult to put two and two together. The last name on the class roster matched the last name in the headlines. I lived in the same district as the one where Dad was arrested. And I closely resembled the photo of him that they used on the news. I was terrified that if my teachers figured out that I was the daughter of a vicious gangster, I would be treated like a criminal, too.

When I enrolled in first grade at public school, they placed me in ESL (English as a second language), even though Mom insisted that my English was sufficient. In fact, I knew English so well that I was beginning to forget my Cantonese and Vietnamese.

The principal, a man in his fifties with a receding hairline and a five o'clock shadow, rolled up the sleeves of his pastel blue button-up shirt as he examined my paperwork. He looked up and studied me and then Mom.

"She doesn't have any school records," he said, poking the papers.

I didn't have any because I hadn't been going to school, aside from those first autumn months in prekindergarten while living with my grandparents. I never went back after I was reunited with my parents when they returned from Canada. There were occasional episodes of kindergarten when we stayed put in Massachusetts, but they didn't last long enough to produce any substantial records.

During one of those episodes, I had a teacher named Mrs. Flanagan, an old woman with copper red hair, a double chin that sagged like a turkey's gobble, and a head that never stopped bobbing up and down.

"Who knows what letter George Washington begins with?" She ignored the hands in the air. "Felicia, what letter does 'George Washington' begin with?" I was a severely timid student. When I didn't immediately respond, she prompted, "Now, let's think about it. Guh-guh-guh George." Her head bobbed harder.

Her enunciation confused me, and I panicked. "J?"

Mrs. Flanagan burst into laughter and the class followed suit.

"Oh, come on, I practically gave you the answer. G! 'George' starts with the letter G, right, everyone?"

I flushed with warmth and looked down at my hands, wishing I was invisible. All I could picture was Mrs. Flanagan stroking a black cat with glowing lime-green eyes when she was at home because she was really a witch and not a teacher. I drowned out the cackling and promised myself I would never make that mistake again.

Mr. Collins was the other teacher I had when I was temporarily in school. He was a tall, slender Black man with a broad, inviting smile. His big teeth were so bright that whenever he smiled, his skin looked darker. One day, we were working on learning to write the alphabet, which I was already an expert in. As the other kids practiced forming their letters, I decided to create art with mine. I curled the ends of the S into whimsical doodles that sprouted flowers and crossed my X in an asymmetric pattern to swordlike points that sprung into fireworks. Enthralled by the process as I waited for the other students to complete their assignments, I didn't pay attention to any lessons taught thereafter.

Mr. Collins took a seat next to me as the kids were dismissed for lunch. "That looks really nice, Felicia," he said from the child-sized chair, his knees bent up to his chest.

"Thanks," I said, showing him the rest of my worksheet.

"But you can't spend the entire day on handwriting. There are other subjects to learn. Why don't we stop here and pick it up another day so you can join the rest of the class? I'm sure you'll improve, and it won't take you this long next time."

I closed the workbook and grimaced behind his back. I

didn't stay long enough to show him that my activity was a result of boredom and not because I was incapable.

Now, the principal sat there, blinking at us in exaggeration, his elbows propped on his wooden desk, expecting us to explain ourselves.

"We moved around a lot," Mom said.

He suggested I take an aptitude test to make sure I started in the appropriate grade. I breezed through it, proving more than ready to begin first grade. Nevertheless, he scheduled ESL into my curriculum. When Mom asked why, he stared at us. I wondered what he saw in us—a young mother with a foreign accent and her mute daughter in an oversized shirt and pants wearing frayed sneakers sitting before him.

"I think it's better to start with it than without it. If we find out that she doesn't need it, she can always drop it later," the principal said before showing us out of his office.

In the spring of that school year, I won the first-grade spelling bee, yet I was still forced to sit through an hour every day in which my teachers treated me as if I couldn't speak English.

I had not made a single friend since enrolling in elementary school four years earlier. But I hadn't minded the lack of friends until the bullying continued through second grade and into my third-grade year. That's when I realized that I had no one to defend me and no one to confide in. Aside from the racial slurs I endured for being one of the only Asian American students in the school, I was teased for wearing the same clothes almost every day and for being ugly. Boys dared to approach me, yapping nonsense, pretending they were speaking Chinese. Girls shoved me into lockers and told me that I looked like a boy. After a teacher coerced me into going to recess, I was knocked unconscious when some kids pushed a metal swing at me and hit me in the head. I was wary of everyone to the point where I once wet myself because I was afraid to ask permission to go to the bathroom.

On a more promising note, I was making flawless grades. The only things that felt safe were library books and calculators. Stories helped me escape my own reality, and the characters I read about were the closest thing I had to socialization. My favorite collection was *Goosebumps* by R. L. Stine, which were all horror fiction stories. There was a kid in each book who was afraid of a monster or a ghost or a puppet or a basement, but the recurring theme was that the child used their wit or imagination to conquer their fears and prevail over evil. As outlandish as some of the plots were, I wanted my story to mirror theirs. Math, on the other hand, brought out my ability to focus and concentrate. I found numbers fascinating. The process of problem-solving was profoundly gratifying compared to the helplessness I felt about many of the real problems I faced. There was only one right answer, and it was one that I could predictably arrive at if I did everything I was supposed to.

I focused on schoolwork and found it therapeutic. Studying became my coping mechanism in so many ways. It distracted me from dwelling on our situation, offered me intellectual confidence, and, with my eyes down on the desk or nose in a book, I evaded some, though not all, of the potential bullying.

"What's that on your hand?" A girl appeared out of nowhere in the cafeteria one day and hovered over me as I was eating. She had long dirty-blonde hair held back with a purple and yellow headband.

"It's a scar." I glanced at my hand nonchalantly. "I got burned by an iron by accident when I was two." I was now eight, accustomed to the discoloration and leatherlike skin that stretched on across the back of my hand from my fingertips to the bend of my wrist and noticed it only when others did.

"Ew. It looks gross," she said, clearly disgusted. She walked away to her friends.

At the end of our lunch break, I was taking my tray to the garbage before joining the rest of my classmates in a single-file line when I heard, "Felicia is so ugly that her own parents burned her with an iron!" The girl who spoke said it as I passed, loud enough to be obvious.

Her four friends snickered, and another chimed in, "They burned her to try to make her prettier, but it didn't work!"

My face reddened as I got in line. I tugged my sleeve over my right hand and ignored them as I waited for the students in front of me to start exiting the cafeteria. The line to leave had never felt so drawn out.

Over the course of my childhood years into adulthood, those comments remained some of the cruelest I had ever heard directed toward me.

Mom once told me about the incident when I burned my hand. She came running into the room so quickly when she heard my cry. She dropped the clothes and hangers she was holding when she saw me sitting under the ironing board with the iron flat on the back of my hand. The smell of burning flesh made her gag as she cleaved the hot metal away. A layer of skin remained adhered to the steaming surface. She called out to Dad's mother for help. When Maa-Maa saw what had happened, she berated Mom in Chinese and grabbed a bag of frozen peas to place over the injury. When I didn't calm down and grew even more inconsolable, Maa-Maa suggested that Mom drive me over to the house of a Vietnamese doctor she knew.

Mom knocked on the doctor's door, and we were quickly ushered inside so he could examine the burn more carefully. He gathered his supplies, which included cream and a bottle of green herbal oil. He recommended that Mom apply the ointment to the lesion, let it air out as much as possible, and rub raw egg whites on the area once it started to scar over.

"That's all?" Mom was dumbfounded.

I continued to cry. When we got back in the car, Mom sped straight to the nearest emergency room.

I was admitted to the hospital.

A day later, I went in for surgery. The doctors performed a skin graft, reallocating skin from my buttock to my hand.

As she sat idle in my hospital room during the operation, two women in business attire and lanyards came in and introduced themselves as DCF workers. One lady interviewed Mom and the other took notes as they repeatedly questioned her about the details of my burn, staggering through her accent.

"Thank you for your time, Ms. Thai," the interviewer said as the other closed the folder and slipped the pen into her shirt pocket.

They walked out, the clack of their heels gradually petering out down the hallway. They never contacted Mom again.

After school one day, I scoured the apartment for another set of clothes. Nothing in Mom's closet fit me, and Amanda's clothes were too childish. I was stuck with the three outfits I had. I tried wearing them in various combinations, used a belt, and rolled the sleeves all the way up to see if they could be disguised as different clothing. I knew I wasn't fooling anyone. Defeated, I took a good look at myself in the full-length mirror. I sat down cross-legged, got closer, and examined myself.

I may have been embarrassed and frightened by the kids at school, but my feelings weren't hurt. Nothing they said made me feel sadness. Perhaps I was desensitized, but somehow my sense of self was intact. Bullying became a nuisance that came along with school, and not a bully in the world could scare me away from attending. The structure, the schedule, and the scholarly stimulation offered me a form of healing. My inherent need for recovery outweighed the petty harassment. These kids had no idea what I had been through. And if they had, they would have understood how ignorant it was to think that teasing me was going to be the way to break me. In isolation, I didn't need friends. I didn't need anybody. In isolation, I realized my strengths and self-worth. I fought to save myself, knowing that no one else would. In isolation, I transformed into my own savior. I would not only survive, but I would flourish as well.

In truth, I found myself to be a pretty girl, and I was quite fond of my features. I thought the angle of my teeth and my unilateral dimple gave me personality. And I liked my light brown eyes and the cheekbones I'd inherited from Dad. Like he always said, I could be Miss Chinatown, and I believed him.

I inspected my face from my forehead to my eyelids, down the bridge of my nose to my chin. "You are beautiful, Felicia," I whispered, "and someday, the world will know that."

23

In January 1998, Dad's trial came to a close.

As his confidants were arrested and interrogated, they were swift to betray him when it became apparent that they, too, were under fire. Some testified against him before the grand jury, painting Dad to be a cold-blooded kingpin. The evidence, the witnesses, and his past all made for a strong prosecution, and in the end, Dad opted for a less severe punishment by accepting a plea bargain.

We turned up the volume on the television as the local news covered the results of the high-profile case. Dad pled guilty on five counts: violent crimes in aid of racketeering activities, conspiracy to commit racketeering activities, aiding and abetting, conspiracy to commit extortion, and conspiracy to commit murder. The judge declared that he would be sentenced to twenty-two years in federal prison. The camera focused on Dad's face, and for an instant, I missed him and wondered if I would ever see him in person again. He appeared unimpressed as he stood next to his lawyer with the same expression I remembered him having when he was being handcuffed in Canada. An officer took Dad into custody, and they retreated from the press.

We lowered the volume again as the view of the courtroom was replaced with the breaking news headline "Guilty plea ends gang terror spree." Mom and I sat inanimate. I was surprisingly indifferent. For as intense as the trial was, the verdict was anti-climactic. I wanted to feel some sort of emotion, whether it be despair or frustration or even contentment, but my heart was hollow. I didn't care. Amanda and Bryan were oblivious, as they should've been. Finally, Mom turned off the television. We never discussed what it all meant for Dad, for us, and for our future. There was simply an air of relief, as if the same key that locked Dad away had just released us to freedom.

24

I fully expected the calls from prison to continue after I hung up with Dad on that fateful day during medical school, but they didn't. After not hearing from him for almost a week, I decided to put it out of my mind for the time being and minimize any distractions by refraining from telling my family the news until after my exam.

After all, I had barely given Dad any of my energy over the last eighteen years, so what was several more weeks? Before Dad's trial ended, Mom was already preparing to move on. Dad couldn't get to us, and because he and Mom were never married, there were no marital legalities that had to be addressed. During the trial, she was left without a penny and three children to raise. As daunting as her conditions were, Mom saw this as her chance to start life over and the opportunity presented itself as an older man.

As Mom was earning her associate's degree and looking for better work, she had heard from a friend that she had a friend who knew a dentist fairly well who was seeking an assistant in Malden, Massachusetts. Donald Levy also happened to be recently divorced, wealthy, and almost thirty years older than Mom. They were set up to meet, though they were both unclear whether it was a date. He asked to see her again, this time over dinner. From the very first official date, Mom decided to be transparent. "I have three children—two daughters and a boy who's three years old. I won't take any man seriously unless he takes all of us seriously." A few weeks later, our lives were uprooted and upgraded. Donald moved us out of the projects and into his big brick house with a two-car garage and a small pond in the back. He hired her on as his dental assistant and proposed to her six months later.

After they were married, Donald took Mom house hunting, and she decided on a four-thousand-square-foot home with French doors located on a cul-de-sac in Newburyport, a coastal city north of Boston. I started middle school there, where I made my first set of friends, and went on to graduate at the top of my high school class in 2003. I wouldn't move again until it was time to leave for James Madison University (JMU) in Virginia to start college.

JMU was where I thrived and built friendships meant to last a lifetime. I met people with various ethnicities from all over the country who were intelligent, creative, and motivated. The mere task of walking through campus inspired me, and premed classes challenged me. I sat in an auditorium of over two hundred freshmen as the biochemistry professor told us that his best guess was that five of us would pass the premed track, get accepted into medical school, earn a residency spot, and become doctors someday. My eyes darted around the classroom, searching for the other four.

Medical school was an obvious decision. It guaranteed me prestige, job security, financial stability, and cerebral invigoration, a predictable pathway toward professional success. More notably, I wanted to make Mom proud, not of me but of herself—undeniable pride in her ability to overcome her personal hardships and her determination to rise up against Dad's worst intentions. Undeniable pride in her fierce perseverance in pursuing something better for us. I wanted Mom to be able to remind herself that she survived as an abused, poor, teenage mother with no support or resources as a non-English-speaking immigrant, and that her resilience had shaped her three children's stories, which could have been doomed for disadvantage, into tales of triumph.

I told Mom first.

"Are you sure?" she asked.

"That's what he said."

"Well, do Amanda and Bryan know?"

"Not yet. I'm planning to tell them. I don't really know what to say, though. It's not like they were old enough to remember him."

"Amanda might remember a little bit. Definitely not Bryan, though. He was just a baby."

I nodded in agreement as if Mom could see me over the phone. "I should tell them, right? He's going to want to see them."

"Yeah, they should know."

I was expecting more of a reaction out of her.

"And you're okay with that?" I asked. "With us talking to him and seeing him and stuff?"

"Yes, Felicia. You're all adults now, so whatever relationship you guys decide to have with Peter, that's up to you. It's none of my business," she said. "He's their father, so they should have the chance to meet him if they want to."

My sister's reaction was equally casual.

When I asked Amanda if she had any memories of Dad, she said, "He would always clean my ear with a Q-tip on a black leather couch. Besides that, not really." She shrugged. "But sure, I'll see him when he gets out, if he wants."

Bryan was entering his senior year in high school when I informed him. "Really? I'd love to meet my dad, see what he's like." He was interested but not overflowing with enthusiasm. "It would be pretty cool to have a dad," Bryan said, as if he were thinking out loud.

After they gave me permission, I relayed their personal cell numbers to Dad so that he could reach out to them. I began to ask myself if I was the only person who felt the burden of Dad's impending presence. Perhaps I had to let go of my childhood grudge against him. After all, it had been eighteen years ago, plenty of years for me to heal and for Dad to change. "The past is trash" was Mom's motto. She was always reminding us to let go of the negativity behind us and revel in another day. Maybe that was the appropriate approach to our situation: forget the past, forgive his faults, and move forward.

Convincing myself of this felt unnatural, mostly because Dad didn't merit any mercy when he was locked up in a prison cell to decay for the duration of his twenty-two-year sentence. No visits, no Father's Day cards, no phone calls, and no annual school portraits. Yet now Dad was granted early freedom, and though he'd never uttered an apology, I was supposed to pick up from where we left off as father and daughter in an imaginary place of normalcy. I wanted to hold up two middle fingers to that idea. *Fuck that. You're a deadbeat dad, and you don't deserve shit.*

The universe had dealt me an unfair twist of fate. I deserved a dad even though he didn't deserve me as a daughter. And in a matter of months, the biological father named on my birth certificate would be there in flesh and blood ready to make up for lost time and promises. Delusions of Dad bringing me flowers on the day of my medical school graduation and making a toast at my wedding were awkward but satisfying. But he just wasn't good enough. So should I settle for him or no father figure at all?

25

wasn't in the proper headspace for any of it. Not Dad's home-coming. Not medical school. Not my family dynamics. And certainly not the resurgence of my childhood memories. I had an intense urge to escape the inevitable, similar to Mom's impulse when she flew to Vietnam. Like her, I needed to leave, clear my psyche, and rejuvenate myself.

I booked a flight to Spain for an eight-day solo trip with half the time spent in Madrid and the other half in Barcelona. There was a deal for a five-hundred-dollar round-trip flight to Madrid, which was affordable on my student loans. I packed light and left two days after my exam late in the spring. When I landed in Madrid, I was already appreciating a bit of reprieve. Nobody knew who I was, which meant there were no expectations or presumptive notions of me, my past, or my future. The scenery, the architecture, and the landscape were all unfamiliar to me. I could barely speak the language, and I couldn't be reached by cell phone or email. It was perfect. I spent entire days roaming through city parks and immersing myself in art, admiring *Las Meninas* in Museo del Prado and Picasso's *Guernica* for hours. I ate breakfast, lunch, and dinner at a table for one and rode the train to Barcelona, sipping my coffee in silence. I got lost in the intricacies of the Sagrada Familia. I forgot the past.

On my last day in Barcelona, I strolled down La Rambla, a famous pedestrian street marked with mosaics in the pavement, souvenir kiosks, street performers, and crowds of tourists. I eventually stopped on a bench with my pistachio ice cream. A Bohemian woman in buoyant gaucho pants and dreadlocks was kneeling on the street beside me, painting on a canvas. I observed as she manipulated vibrant colors into the wings of a bird in flight. I complimented her on her talent.

"Gracias," she said, looking up at me on the bench. "What brings you to Barcelona?"

"No reason in particular," I said. "I just needed to get away from home, be in a new place."

"You made a great choice, my friend. Is anyone traveling with you?"

"Nope. I'm by myself. It's actually really refreshing," I said, tilting my head and looking around us.

"Wow. Good for you." She beamed at me and then went back to painting. Her wrist full of bracelets jangled with each brush stroke as she created more magic in the feathers. "Do you know what kind of bird this is?" she asked.

"It's beautiful. Looks like a hummingbird, no?"

"It is! Yes. Do you know what hummingbirds symbolize?"

"I don't."

She paused from her artwork again, her eyes bright.

"Joy and happiness. Their colors bring positivity and love. They're healers. No matter what you might be going through, my friend, the spirit of a hummingbird will guide you."

26

The essence of Spain was the idyllic respite from the forth-coming drama. I returned to medical school in time to start clinical rotations at the local healthcare facilities. As Dad's tentative release date grew closer, the frequency of his calls increased, as did my efforts to cope. A cascade of childhood memories clashed with my adult interpretation. I stumbled through my feelings, trying to balance pain and perspective. The process began with finding empathy for my father and seeking justifications to explain his behavior and his impropriety.

I rationalized it to myself like this: Dad suffered trauma during the Vietnam War. He endured more of it in the Malaysian refugee camp. He was poor. He was an immigrant. He needed work. He needed money. He entered the underworld as a means to an end, and leaving a life of crime wasn't easy. He made mistakes. He experienced the consequences. He spent eighteen years in custody rehabilitating himself, losing his wife and children in the process. He loved with a preposterous amount of complexity. He deserved a second chance, and I had the power to grant that.

I started by calling him "Dad" again. I never addressed him as Peter, but I had stopped calling him anything after he was sentenced. "Dad" was a meaningful word filled with endearment and expectations, which felt unsuitable for him. As uncomfortable as it was, I figured the practice would normalize like everything else that gradually transitioned into habit. Yet each time I heard myself use that intimate term, it sounded like someone else was saying it. It was as if I saw a stranger in the street drop his keys, chased after him down the sidewalk, tapped him on the shoulder to return them, and called this man "Dad" when he turned to me. It felt wrong. Nevertheless, I persisted, deeming myself ungrateful and asking myself how many fatherless daughters wished for an opportunity to rekindle a relationship like that. I let my guard down and opened up by sharing my personal life with Dad, one disclosure at a time.

When Dad asked what type of doctor I would become after medical school, I said, "I don't know yet. I really like to work with my hands, so I'm thinking probably surgery or anesthesia. Something in the operating room."

"And how much money does a doctor like that make?"

I assured him that it was enough to take care of myself.

When I spit out an approximated salary, he scoffed. "Per year? I was making that in months. It's not that much money. And how much does it cost to go to medical school?" He was flabbergasted when I told him the amount of debt I was accumulating. "Wow. Doesn't seem like it's worth it."

I was confused; there was nothing but disappointment in his tone. Yet I was a first-generation daughter of Chinese and Vietnamese immigrants and destined to become a physician. There was a disconnect somewhere, perhaps between our generations or culture or lifestyle. I wasn't sure, but I attributed it to him being an overly concerned father. He wanted more for me.

"Do you have a boyfriend?"

I started telling Dad about a guy I had been seeing while studying in Miami.

"He treats you good?"

I reassured him that he treated me well and that we had a lot of fun together.

"Okay, baby. As long as he's good to you. That's good. You tell your daddy if any guy treats you bad, okay?"

I chuckled, secretly relishing the idea of having an overprotective father.

"So he's Asian? Chinese like your daddy? He's an Asian guy, right?"

"I didn't say that," I hedged.

"Okay, so is he a White boy?"

"I didn't say that, either."

"Oh, not White, either? So what is he? Indian? Spanish? Black? What?"

"He's Black."

He paused.

"You're dating a Black guy?"

"Yes, Dad. I am."

Racism is not uncommon in immigrant Asian communities. Between that and the blatant racism that existed in prison,

I braced myself for whatever he might say next. But he didn't say much of anything and changed the topic.

A few days later, Mom called, asking if I had told Dad I was dating a Black guy. I confirmed, "Yeah, I told him. Why?"

Apparently, Dad had called Mom and launched a verbal attack on how she'd raised me. "She's dating a fucking Black guy," he'd ranted to Mom. "A fucking lowlife. What did you do while I was away, Lon? Felicia doesn't speak Chinese anymore. She doesn't speak Vietnamese. She doesn't know shit about her own culture. What the fuck did you do to my kids? What kind of mother lets this happen?"

After that, I stopped answering his calls and wrote him a letter:

Dear Peter,

How dare you cast judgment on Mom, me, and who I love? You are the lowlife, a deadbeat dad rotting in a prison cell. You cheated on Mom, and you abused her. I am with someone who is nothing like you. You should be happy for me and how I turned out, especially since you played no part in the woman I've become.

Do not call or write me again unless you plan on accepting whomever I love, regardless of the color of their skin.

Felicia

I began to regret allowing Dad back in my life, allowing him to hurt me again. I was stronger than that, I told myself. After the torment he had put me through—put us through—it was foolish of me to bestow forgiveness for unforgivable behavior.

After I mailed my letter, I didn't hear from Dad for weeks. Rather than managing my emotions, I grew numb. I needed to divert my energy elsewhere, and the demands of medical school were insufficient. So, I started to drink.

I was living in Miami with my three best friends from medical school where we were completing our final semester before starting clinical rotations. Miami was a vibrant city saturated with distractions. Walking a few blocks in any direction led to tropical cocktails, palm trees framing a picture-perfect beach, or a group of sun-kissed souls ready to salsa the night away.

Drinking on the weekends turned into drinking and smoking hookah every night. Going out until dawn turned into sleepless days as I went from the bar to the after-hours nightclub and then home to change before going to pool parties. Hungover from my drinking binges, I urged my roommates to forge my signature on the attendance sheet as I slept through class and showed up only on exam dates. It didn't end there. I started blacking out during these escapades.

"Girl, are you doing okay?" my roommates asked, noticing me spiraling further and further out of control. Jenny, Jessica, and Louise were my best friends. I considered them to be my sisters, really. I had met them at the start of medical school two years earlier, and we had been inseparable since. There was something about the four of us working toward the same ambition under the stress of medical school that made us grow close in a short period of time. We studied together, we ate together, we celebrated together, and then when we had to relocate from the West Indies to Miami for the clinical half of medical school, we moved in together. Medical school went from a potentially tough and taxing four years to some of the most memorable and influential years of my life, all because of these girls.

"I'm fine. It's just a lot going on." I squinted my eyes and forced a smile. I didn't want to talk about what was bothering me because I didn't expect anyone to understand. And I had discovered long ago that I didn't need anyone. Each of them knew snippets of my family dynamics minus the details, just the basics: I was the product of a criminal dad, a struggling mom, and a troubled past. There was little any one of them could do or say that would help, and I held on to the belief that I was my greatest savior. They had more important things to worry about than me. I was going to be fine.

Rather than fly to another country like I had to Spain, I was slipping into the convenience of my own belligerence. On the dance floor, under the influence as blaring hip-hop lyrics oscillated through the speakers, I was safe from my own thoughts. I felt present and only existed when the flashing strobe lights found me. All I cared about was moving my hips to the beat and making sure not to spill Vodka Red Bull on my dress.

My roommates began to worry when I came home morning after morning inebriated, passing out in the clothes I wore the night before and reeking of marijuana and alcohol. After they found me in bed with rigors, covered in cold sweat and vomit, with intractable nausea and diarrhea, the girls debated performing an intervention. They found nips of liquor all over my bedroom and considered throwing them away. They tried to talk to me, but I reiterated that there was nothing to talk about. They reached out to college friends of mine for advice on how to help. "There's nothing to do," one of my closest friends assured my roommates. "Felicia's a renegade. Let her go through it. Trust me. She'll bounce back." They dropped the issue and decided to wait it out.

My bedroom was spinning when the sunlight snuck through the blinds and woke me up one morning. My drinking binges had been going on for weeks on end. I started to pull the covers over my head and realized that I didn't know how I got home that night. I still had an orange wristband from the club. Without that, I wouldn't have known where I went last night either. I fumbled through my clutch, making sure I had my wallet and phone. Instead, I found my car keys, along with a few crumpled dollars and my lipstick.

I ran outside to see my crappy bright yellow Honda Accord with the convertible top detached, parked slanted in the driveway. In awe and barefoot, I walked toward the car unphased by the hot tar driveway. I had no recollection of driving home the night before. My phone was underneath the driver seat with calls and text messages to people I must have met while I was out. I crept back into the house.

Before I got to my room, one of my roommates stepped out into the hallway with her hands on her hips and her cheeks sucked in. "I could hear you guys all night," she said, pointing downstairs. "You might be done with your exam, but the rest of us are still studying."

"Shit. Sorry," I apologized, racking my brain as to what kind of noise we were making after I supposedly drove us here. I later learned that I had invited a group of people over after leaving the nightclub and that we had caused a ruckus until almost 4:00 a.m.

"So inconsiderate, Felicia," she huffed and rolled her eyes.

I stood there, without a word. I knew she was right. She shook her head and slammed the bedroom door behind her.

I went to take a shower. The water pattered against the tub as I took my earrings out and got undressed. I looked in the mirror. My head was throbbing. Leftover makeup was smeared across my cheeks. Smokey eyeshadow and eyeliner streaked into an uneven discoloration, and my mascara was clumped at the tip of my lashes. The curls in my hair were matted together and stiff from dried-out mousse. I rubbed my neck as I bent my head from one side to another. My face went out of focus as the steam condensed over my reflection.

I showered in disappointment, trying to wash away the odor of shame. I needed to snap out of this. I lathered my hair in conditioner, undoing the tangles from the roots to the ends. I couldn't avoid the agony that resurfaced from the past anymore. I had to face it, tackle it, and overcome it before it wasted all of the effort I had invested into becoming the woman I was and destroyed me. I scrubbed myself with a loofah, and the filth circled down the drain. I wouldn't let any of it jeopardize my future.

By the time the summer semester ended in September, I had reorganized my clinical rotation schedule, relocating myself to hospitals and clinics in various cities. The academic portion of medical school was finished, and each clinical rotation varied from two weeks to three months depending on whether it was a core field or an elective. I chose sites with the strongest reputations in the specialties I had interests in, which landed me first in Baltimore; then in Cape Cod, Brooklyn, and the Bronx; and later, temporarily back in Miami. It was also a way to remove my vulnerability and enter environments less conducive to reckless behavior.

I drove my lemon of a car to Baltimore.

Sorrow leaked into my sober thoughts again. This time, though, I channeled it into motivation, excelling as a medical student at Harbor Hospital in Baltimore and getting fit. I limited my drinking to the weekends and cut back on my intake. My work ethic was being recognized as I spent my time outside of the hospital preparing for my patients and reading relevant material for didactic sessions. At the sessions, we discussed patient cases and expanded on learning objectives from them. I was an energetic participant and responded with correct answers and well-thought-out explanations. I was back in the gym and handling my stress with spin classes and kickboxing.

I didn't speak to anyone about what was happening inside me. Again, in isolation was where I expected to overcome any and all obstacles. It wasn't as if I debated reaching out for help. That strategy did not exist to me. And even if it did, there was no one to reach out to. No one would understand me, let alone empathize with me, and the energy it would require to tell my story in a meaningful way would take away from the energy I needed to get through this. The exhaustion from the questions, the unknowns, the dysfunction, the hypotheticals, and the emotions was potentially detrimental to my tenacity. I couldn't risk that. I was doing well, staying strong, but sometimes, the entire thing felt unfair. It seemed as though Mom couldn't care less about Dad's release. She had moved on so far forward and was so far removed from her past that the residual effects couldn't touch her. As for Amanda and Bryan, they did not have a single significant memory of Dad. Thus, they had no grudges and no regrets, just an untainted opportunity to reconcile with him.

During the months I spent in Baltimore, I also fell in love with a classmate. Ricky Daniel Heath Jr. was handsome and intelligent, quiet and confident. There were layers to his character. I gravitated toward him, my intuition telling me that I would soon realize he was my soulmate. He became even more than that. I let my guard down and opened up to him.

Late one evening, we had finished dinner, lit candles, and were lying on the floor of a cheap apartment without any furniture besides an air mattress. Ricky asked about my family. When he asked about my dad, I cried. I sobbed as I described the kind of man he was and how many years it had been since I had seen him last. I planted my forehead into the carpet, trying to stop the tears after confessing how much I wished for a real dad. I had never said that to anyone before. It was as if I were an actress on set, but the cameras were off, the stage was empty, and the crew had gone home. I was given permission to be human, and in this safe space, I didn't have to put on a show. Ricky lifted my head onto his chest and rubbed my back until the candles went out.

Before long, I heard from Dad again. I listened as he attempted an apology. "Whoever you want to be with, I'm okay with that. Okay, baby? If he treats you good, then I'll treat him good."

"Okay, good, because I'm with someone, and he's not Asian."

"Fine. That's fine with me. Asian or not Asian, it doesn't matter to me, okay? I love you," he said. "Can I meet him when I get out? Daddy wants to meet this guy."

We resumed communication, and Dad was again calling about once a week. He updated me on his health, his tentative release date, and his plans for after prison. I tried to limit the details of my personal life that I shared and not make the mistake of getting hurt like before. We kept our conversations brief, eliminating any room for drama.

He was also calling Amanda and Bryan on a regular basis. With time, they both developed their own unique relationships with Dad. As their keeper, I vowed to myself to provide as little or as much guidance as they needed throughout this delicate affair, trying to find a balance between keeping my input neutral and also keeping Dad accountable.

27

I was the last to arrive for dinner. Parking was scarce close to 6:00 p.m. in Boston's Italian district, so Ricky drove around the block until we found a spot nearby.

Dad had been released two months earlier, but between all our separate lives, it had taken this long to coordinate a night when we could conveniently get together. There was a break between the end of medical school rotations and the official graduation date, so Ricky and I were in Brockton, Massachusetts, visiting his family. I called Dad to let him know that we were on our way as Ricky looked for change to feed the meter. That done, I put my phone in my purse, unbuckled my seat belt, and took a deep breath.

"Okay, are you ready?" Ricky asked, holding my hand. His wistful chestnut eyes focused on me as if he was worried.

"I'm ready," I said, squeezing his hand. "Thanks for agreeing to come tonight."

We had reservations at Fiore. Dad was waiting for us by the hostess stand, wide-eyed and overzealous, in his wire-framed glasses and gold tie.

"Wow, look at you!" Dad said when he caught sight of me, as if I had just undergone a complete, life-altering makeover. "You're beautiful, baby."

He gave me a hug. When we let go, he held me straight out by my arms to take another thorough look at me. "You still look like your daddy, though, huh?" He smirked and showed us to the table.

The aroma of pesto and fresh bread filled the restaurant as the waitstaff uncorked bottles of Chianti and grated blocks of Parmesan cheese. Ricky and I hugged Mom, Amanda, and Bryan before taking a seat at the round table. With each embrace, I tried to remember the last time that each of us had seen Dad. He reached across me to shake Ricky's hand when I introduced them and then waved the waiter over to take his drink order. We browsed the menu in awkward silence as Dad requested every appetizer they offered.

"So, Felicia," he said, closing the menu. "How are you? Tell me everything."

EPILOGUE

During the next two months after our reunion at Fiore, I finished my last year of medical school and graduated with my medical degree. I went on to become a critical care anesthesiologist, a career that has blossomed from the chaos we endured during my childhood, allowing me to bring stability to the hospital's most acute patients on an everyday basis. Over the years, I have leaked my story to colleagues, friends, mentors, and on social media, speaking candidly when the opportunity exposed itself. Outside of the prison cell and in living color, Dad became relevant. I decided to tell my truth rather than give vague and ambiguous accounts when asked about my family. In candor and in humility, I found power in my story.

I entertained my relationship with Dad for about a year with regular phone calls and occasional visits. During the course of that year, my interactions with him felt forced and inauthentic. The initial enthusiasm vanished, and I peacefully came to terms with my lack of desire to have Dad in my life in a significant way. We have mainly gone our separate ways, but he continues to be a father to Amanda and Bryan. Amanda lives in Northern Virginia and is thriving in all areas of her life both professional and personal. She developed the closest relationship to Dad. Bryan lives on the beach in New Hampshire, enjoying each day as it unfolds. The father-son dynamic between them is complicated and unsatisfying, a battle of uncertain expectations with no resolution in sight.

Dad is now a grandfather to my three children, and I make sure to set aside time for them to see him whenever we are near Boston. I married Ricky like I knew I would, and we have a fourth child due to enter the world months prior to the set publication date of this book. My husband and growing family fulfill me in every way that my childhood didn't.

Before Dad's release, I knew almost nothing about my mom. Dad's newfound presence complicated my relationship with her. I could not understand how she could be around someone who had hurt and disrespected her in the ways he had. Ironically, the complexity of the circumstances allowed for conversations between us that don't often occur among Asian immigrant parents and their first-generation American children. Recognizing generational trauma and becoming a mother myself helped me accept and better appreciate Mom's past and the decisions she made. Her story remains the most important narrative in the book and a tremendous inspiration for me writing *Spirit of a Hummingbird*.

I can't remember the last time the five of us were together since Fiore. Perhaps it was a few times before life went on. A few more shifts in karma. A few more heartfelt attempts at fitting ourselves into a family. A few more second chances to sit down and eat dinner like we were once supposed to. A few more chances to look at it all for what it was, hold on to the value it has brought to my growth, and let the rest go. There's not much more I could ask for in this lifetime.

ABOUT THE AUTHOR

Photo by Vanessa Guevara

FELICIA HEATH is a triple-board-certified critical care anesthesiologist, blogger, and debut author. She spent a month alone in a studio in the heart of Philadelphia to write the original manuscript of *Spirit of a Hummingbird: Memories from a Childhood on the Run*, just seventy-two hours after delivering her third child. This left her husband with their two-year-old, one-year-old, and newborn as she drank pinot noir and wrote for days on end. All of it was his idea, which is exactly why she tattooed his name across her shoulder and eloped with him on a South African safari six years ago. Felicia now lives in Pennsylvania with her husband and four children. She practices medicine as she anticipates a shift in the universe with the release of her memoir.

Visit Felicia's blog, at www.mixedfeelingsmama.com, to learn more about her purpose.